Many thanks to the great restaurants and chefs for sharing these wonderful recipes with everyone. These great dishes will be enjoyed by all.

Dedicated to the victims of Hurricane Katrina

D. Levert

Cover Photo courtesy PDPHOTO.ORG
Back Cover Photos © Roy Tennant, FreeLargePhotos.com

CHAPTER 1 _____ SOUPS _____ Page 7

CHAPTER 2 _____ APPETIZERS _____ Page 23

CHAPTER 3 _____ SALADS _____ Page 43

CHAPTER 4 _____ SIDE DISHES _____ Page 54

CHAPTER 5 _____ ENTREES _____ Page 66

Historical French Quarter
Photo © Roy Tennant, FreeLargePhotos.com

StreetCar in New Orleans
Photo © Roy Tennant, FreeLargePhotos.com

Commander's Palace Restaurant
Photo © Roy Tennant, FreeLargePhotos.com

Swamp in Houma near New Orleans
Photo © Roy Tennant, FreeLargePhoto

CHAPTER 1

SOUPS

Louisiana Crab and Corn Bisque (From 'Cooking Creole', Marcelle Bienvenu)
Makes 6 servings

2 tablespoons butter
1 cup chopped onions
1/4 cup chopped red bell peppers
1/2 cup chopped green bell peppers
1/2 cup chopped celery
1 tablespoon minced garlic
2 cups shrimp stock or chicken broth
1/2 cup dry white wine
1/2 teaspoon dried thyme
1/4 cup vegetable oil
1/4 cup all-purpose flour
3 1/2 cups heavy cream
1 teaspoon salt
1 teaspoon hot sauce
1 1/2 cups fresh corn kernels
1 pound lump crabmeat, picked over
for shells and cartilage
1 tablespoon chopped parsley
1 tablespoon chopped green onions
16 jumbo crab claws (optional)

Heat the butter in a large saucepan over medium heat. Add the onions, peppers, celery and garlic, and cook, stirring, 1 minute. Add the stock, wine and thyme, and bring to a boil.
In a skillet over medium heat combine the oil and flour and, stirring constantly, make a blond roux. Add the roux to the mixture in the
saucepan and mix well to blend. Reduce the heat to medium-low. Add the cream in a steady stream, whisking with a wire whisk to combine the mixture. Add the salt, hot sauce and the corn. Simmer for 5 minutes.
Add the crabmeat, parsley and green onions, and cook for about 5 minutes, or until the soup is well heated. To serve, garnish with crab claws.

Crab and Mushroom Bisque (From Chef Keegan)

10 cups fish or seafood stock
(or, in a pinch, bottled clam juice)
1 cup (2 sticks) butter
1 cup flour
12 ounces mushrooms, sliced
1/2 cup chopped onion
4 whole scallions, sliced
1/2 cup butter (to sauté)
1/4 cup minced Italian parsley
1 cup cream
1 cup half-and-half
1/2 cup dry Sherry
1/4 teaspoon cayenne pepper
1/2 teaspoon white pepper
1 teaspoon salt
4 1/2 cups (1 pound) lump crabmeat
1/4 cup Parmesan cheese

Melt 1 stick butter and in it sauté onions, mushrooms and scallions until tender. While sautéing bring fish stock to a boil. Put all sautéed vegetables and 4 cups hot stock in blender (in batches) and purée until smooth.
Make a roux using 1 cup butter and 1 cup flour. Add 4 cups stock (hot) and puréed vegetable mixture whisking constantly. Add the remaining stock, continuing to whisk. Turn heat to low. Add all seasonings, half of cream, half-and-half and half of Sherry. Do not allow to boil. (Can be made ahead to this point.)
When ready to finish, reheat but do not boil. Mix in approximately 1/4 cup freshly grated Parmesan, remaining cream, half-and-half and Sherry, and crabmeat. Stir until cheese is melted and crab is heated through. Serves 8.

Crawfish Bisque (From Corinne Dunbar's)

Soup:
2 pounds crawfish
1 pound shrimp
3 quarts water
1 1/2 medium-sized onions
3/4 clove garlic
2 pieces celery
4 sprigs thyme
2 bay leaves
2 cloves (optional)
3 ounces tomato paste
1/2 cup flour
1/4 cup water
1 teaspoon Kitchen Bouquet

Stuffing:
2 tablespoons shortening
1/2 onion
1/4 clove garlic
1 piece celery
2 sprigs thyme
1/8 cup tomato paste
Salt, pepper, and cayenne
1/2 loaf French bread

Soak crawfish 1 hour in strong salted water. Drain, rinse, and drain again. Boil shrimp a few minutes in 1 quart lightly salted water. Remove shrimp, peel, and finely chop. Reserve for stuffing. Put shrimp heads back in water in which shrimp were boiled, add 2 more quarts of water and crawfish. Add the onions, garlic, celery, thyme, bay leaves, cloves and tomato paste. Boil about 30 to 40 minutes, remove crawfish and strain broth. Add flour-water mixture to broth for thickening, and Kitchen Bouquet. Simmer 2 hours, stirring frequently.
To make stuffing: Peel crawfish, saving heads, and chop fine. Combine with chopped shrimp. Simmer about 30 minutes in shortening together with the onion, garlic, celery, thyme and tomato paste. Break up French bread into small pieces, squeeze out after soaking in water, and add to the crawfish, shrimp and seasonings. Simmer about 20 minutes longer, stirring constantly. Let cool, then stuff into the empty shells of crawfish heads. Before serving, the stuffed heads may be browned slightly in a moderate oven. Add 3 or 4 heads to each bowl of soup. Serves 10.

Shrimp Bisque (From The Caribbean Room)

2 pounds shrimp
1 large onion, chopped
2 tablespoons chopped celery
2 tablespoons butter
2 tablespoons flour
2 quarts water
1/2 cup bread crumbs
Salt and pepper

Shrimp Balls:
2 tablespoons chopped green onions
1/8 cup butter [2 tablespoons]
4 tablespoons fine bread crumbs
1 egg yolk

Peel and clean shrimp and run through a neat grinder. Sauté onion and celery in butter, add flour, and cook about 2 minutes. Gradually add water and, when blended, add shrimp. Cook 15 to 20 minutes. Add bread crumbs, cook a few minutes, remove from fire, and strain to separate liquid and shrimp mixture. Set aside half of shrimp mixture for shrimp balls and put the other half back into the soup. Purée, season, and set aside.

To make shrimp balls:
Sauté shallots in butter and add reserved shrimp mixture and bread crumbs. Moisten with 4 tablespoons soup. Remove from fire and beat in egg yolk. Let cool and roll into balls about the size of walnuts. Heat in oven at 350 degrees F. about 5 to 6 minutes. Put at least 2 shrimp balls in each serving. Yield: About 2 quarts soup.

Makes 5 quarts, enough for about 16 entrée servings

Seafood & Okra Gumbo (From Commander's Palace)

3/4 cup vegetable oil
3/4 cup all-purpose flour
3 onions, in medium dice
1 medium bunch celery, in medium dice
6 medium cloves garlic, peeled and minced
1 teaspoon cayenne pepper, or to taste
Pinch of dried oregano
Pinch of dried basil
Pinch of dried thyme
4 bay leaves, preferably fresh
Kosher salt and freshly ground pepper to taste
2 quarts cold water
1 1/2 pounds gumbo crabs or blue crabs
(hard-shell tops off, gill removed, cut in half,
with claws cracked with back of knife)
1 pound andouille sausage, sliced in
1/4-inch rounds (sausage should be smoked and
firm; other smoked sausage can be substituted)
1/4 pound okra, tops removed, in 1/8-inch-thick rings
1 pound medium shrimp, peeled and deveined, tails on
1 quart shucked oysters, in their liquor
Hot sauce to taste
Boiled rice
3 green onions, thinly sliced

Pour the oil into a heavy, dry stockpot with a capacity of at least 8 quarts, and heat the oil until it is very hot. Make a roux by slowly adding the flour and stirring constantly with a wooden spoon for about 3 to 5 minutes, until the mixture is the color of milk chocolate. Scraping the sides of the pot and stirring constantly are the key to a good roux. Be careful not to burn the roux; if black spots appear, it will be unusable and you will need to start over. Once roux is the proper color, add the onions, cook for 1 minute, add the celery, and cook for 30 seconds. Add the bell pepper and scrape the bottom of the pot. The aroma should be slightly burned and very appealing. Add the garlic, cayenne, oregano, basil, thyme, bay leaves, salt, and pepper. Add the cold water to the mixture, stirring constantly to prevent lumps. Add the crabs and sausage, bring to a boil, then simmer, uncovered, for 45 minutes, skimming constantly and stirring occasionally to avoid sticking. Add the okra and cook for 15 minutes more, skimming off any fat. Stir gently so as not to break up the okra. Add the shrimp, the oysters, and the oyster liquor, and bring to a boil. Reduce the heat and simmer >

for 10 minutes. Finish the soup with your favorite Louisiana hot sauce, then adjust the salt and pepper to taste. Serve over rice, and garnish with the green onions.
Tip: Skimming gumbos is essential to a good, clean shine.
You may want to adjust consistency by adding more water to thin it or simmering to thicken it.

Oyster and Artichoke Soup (From Chef Warren Leruth)

- 4 fresh artichokes
- 1 pint of oysters
- 1 quart oyster water (if available)
- 1 lemon, quartered
- 1 small onion, sliced
- 2 sprigs fresh thyme
- 2 bay leaves
- 1 tsp. salt 1/4 tsp. pepper
- 1/2 stick butter
- 2 Tbs. flour
- 1/2 tsp. Tabasco

1. Wash and trim the hard ends of the leaves of the artichokes, and remove all bruised leaves. Cut the artichokes in half.
2. Drain the oysters and rinse them. Strain and save all the oyster water, and add enough plain water to make six cups in a saucepan. Add the artichokes, lemon, onion, thyme, bay leaves, salt, and pepper. Simmer for 40 minutes.
3. Remove artichokes from the liquid. When cool, remove leaves, separate hearts and bottoms, and dispose of the choke. In a food processor or blender, puree the soft meat from the leaves. Pull apart the hearts. Dice the bottoms finely.
4. Make a light roux from the butter and flour. Whisk this into the liquid and return to a boil. Add the pureed artichokes and boil for 10 minutes.
5. Chop the oysters coarsely, reserving a dozen the big, good-looking ones.
6. Strain soup through a fine sieve into a clean pot. Add the chopped oysters, the leaves from the hearts, the diced artichoke bottoms, salt and Tabasco to taste. Heat to a simmer, then add the whole oysters. Simmer two more minutes, then serve.

Serves six.

Creole Crawfish and Tasso Chowder (From The Bombay Club Restaurant)

Ingredients:
½ c. Salad oil
½ lb. Bacon, diced
1 cup Tasso, finely diced
1 Large Onion, diced
3 Celery stalks, diced
1 large carrot, diced
1 ea. Red and Green Peppers, diced
2 ears Corn, remove kernels from ears
1 Tbs. Tarragon, Thyme, Kosher Salt
1 ½ Tbs. Garlic, minced
2 tsp. Fresh cracked black pepper
1 ea. Bay leaves, 1 pinch Cayenne pepper
½ c. White wine
¼ c. Worcestershire sauce, 2 dashes Tabasco
1/2 gal. Shrimp stock or broth
1 c. Blonde roux
1 qt. Heavy cream
4 c. Crawfish tails, pre-cooked
3 ea. Russet potatoes, cubed and par-boiled

Directions:

Heat oil in a medium stock pot, add bacon, sauté 3 to 5 minutes or until bacon is slightly crispy. Add Tasso, onions, celery, carrots and peppers, sauté for 5 to 7 minutes. Add corn, garlic, herbs, and spices, sauté another 2 to 3 minutes. Deglaze with white wine, Worcestershire, and Tabasco, simmer for 2-3 minutes. Add shrimp stock, bring to a boil then whisk in roux, stirring well, so no lumps form. Turn down heat and simmer for 5 minutes, add heavy cream, crawfish, and strained potatoes. Simmer for 5 to 10 minutes. Season to taste.

Creole Turtle Soup Recipe (From Mother's Restaurant)

Roux:
1 Cup Unsalted Butter
1/2 Cup All Purpose Flour

4 Tbsp Usalted Butter
1 lb Turtle Meat Cut into 1/2 inch cubes
1 1/2 Cup Onion, Finely Diced
1 Cup Celery, Finely Diced
1/4 Cup Green Onion, Finely Sliced
2 tsp Garlic, Minced
2 Fresh Bay Leaves
1 1/2 Cup Fresh Tomato, Diced
1 Qt Beef Stock
1 Pinch Cayenne
1 Pinch Ground Allspice
2 Tbsp Fresh Thyme Leaves
1 Tbsp Fresh Marjoram, Chopped
Salt and Black Pepper to taste
1/4 Cup Fresh Lemon Juice
4 Tbsp Worcestershire Sauce
3 Tbsp Sherry
3 Hard Boiled Eggs, Whites diced, Yolks Riced
Lemon Slices
5 tsp Italian Pasley, Finely Chopped

Melt the 1 Cup of Butter in a heavy bottomed saucepan, whisk in the flour, cook to make a peanut butter colored Roux. Set aside. For more on making a Roux, click here.
In a large saucepan or dutch oven, melt the 4 Tbsp of Unalted Butter over medium-high heat, add the diced Turtle Meat and saute until nicely browned. Lower the heat to medium, add both types of onions, the celery, and garlic. Season with salt and black pepper. Saute until the vegetables are tender. >
Add the tomatoes, season with a little salt so they will break down, cook for 10 minutes.
Add the Beef Stock, Worcestershire, Cayenne, Allspice, and Bay Leaves. Bring to a boil, then down to a simmer. Simmer for 20-30 minutes, stirring occasionally and skimming off any impurities that may rise to the surface.
Whisk in the Roux, simmer until thickened and smooth. Add the Thyme, and Marjoram, simmer for 15-20 minutes more.
Add the Lemon Juice, 3 tsp of the Parsley, and the riced Egg Yolk, heat through. Serve garnished with Lemon Slices, Diced Egg Whites, and Parsley. Add the Sherry at the table, about 1-2 tsp per bowl. Seves 4-6

Creole Bouillabaisse (From Chef John Folse)

PREP TIME: 1½ Hours
SERVES: 12

INGREDIENTS:

- 4 (1½ pound) cleaned red snapper
- 2 pounds head on shrimp (31-35 count)
- 4 whole bay leaves
- 2 pounds live crawfish
- 12 fresh cleaned crabs
- 1 cup olive oil
- 2 cups chopped onions
- 2 cups chopped celery
- 1 cup chopped red bell pepper
- 4 whole diced tomatoes
- 3/4 cup tomato sauce
- 1/4 cup diced garlic
- 2 medium carrots, diced
- 3 quarts shellfish stock
- 2 cups dry white wine
- 1 tsp dry thyme
- 1 tsp dry basil
- 1 cup sliced green onions
- 1 cup chopped parsley
- salt and cayenne pepper to taste

METHOD:
Pour olive oil into a two-gallon stock pot. Layer the onions, celery, bell pepper, tomatoes, tomato sauce, garlic, bay leaves, and carrots. On top of vegetables, layer whole fish, shrimp, crawfish, and crabs. Place on medium-high heat, cover and steam approximately three to five minutes. Add shellfish stock, white wine, thyme and basil. Bring to a low simmer, approximately 190 degrees F, or just below the boiling point. Top of stock should ripple but not boil. Cook thirty minutes and remove from heat. Carefully pour off all shellfish stock, and reserve for soup. Using a spatula remove all seafood. Peel shrimp, crawfish > and crab, then de-bone all meat from the fish. Bring the stock back to a low boil and add all seafood. Reduce to a simmer and add green onions and parsley. Season to taste using salt and cayenne pepper. Serve by placing a generous amount of the seafood in the center of a soup bowl and ladle over with hot soup.

BUTTERNUT SHRIMP BISQUE (From Brigtsen's)
Yield: 6 servings

Ingredients:
3 Tablespoons unsalted butter
2 cups diced yellow onion
1 bay leaf
4 cups butternut squash (peeled, de-seeded, and diced into ½ - inch cubes)
2 cups peeled fresh shrimp
2 ¼ teaspoons salt
3/8 teaspoon ground cayenne pepper
1/8 teaspoon ground white pepper
½ cup shrimp stock (see NOTE)
6 cups heavy whipping cream

NOTE: To make shrimp stock, place shrimp heads and shells into a saucepan and cover with cold water. Bring to a boil. Reduce heat to low and simmer for 15 minutes. Strain.

1. Heat the butter in a heavy-duty saucepan over medium-high heat. Add the onions and bay leaf and cook, stirring constantly, until the onions become soft and clear, 3- 4 minutes.
2. Reduce heat to medium and add the butternut squash. Cook this mixture, stirring occasionally, until the squash begins to soften, 6-8 minutes.
3. Reduce heat to low and add the shrimp, salt, cayenne, and white pepper. Cook, stirring occasionally, until the shrimp turn pink, 2-3 minutes.
4. Add the shrimp stock and cook, stirring occasionally, for 6-8 minutes. If the mixture begins to stick to the pan, scrape it with a spoon and continue cooking. This will intensify the flavor of the bisque.
5. Remove bay leaf and discard. Transfer the squash/shrimp mixture to a food processor and puree. Return the puree to a saucepan and add the cream. Whisk until thoroughly blended. Bring to a boil. Reduce heat to low and simmer for 2-3 minutes.

Oysters and Brie Cheese Soup (From P & J Oyster Company)
Ingredients:
2 Pints Oysters
4 toes garlic (chopped)
4 Tablespoons Butter
1 bunch green onions (chopped)
1 pint heavy cream
oyster liquor
1/2 chopped onions
2 Tbsp. lemon juice
1 pint half & half
1 wedge brie cheese
1/4 cup flour
1/4 cup chopped parsley
salt and pepper

Instructions:
In large pan, sauté garlic and green onions. Put oysters in 4 quart pot and simmer until oysters curl and take off heat. Stir in brie cheese and heavy cream to sautéed vegetables. Keep stirring on medium-high flame until cheese melts. (This will thicken soup sauce) Add oysters and oyster liquor and simmer. Add half and half and heat on low flame for 5 minutes stirring occasionally.

Oyster and Eggplant Soup (P & J Oyster Company)

Ingredients
1 pint raw oysters
2 medium eggplant
2 cup oyster liqueur
4 large cloves of garlic
2 rib celery
1 cup heavy cream
4 Tbsp. butter
2 Tbsp. flour
Salt and pepper to taste

Instructions
Peel eggplant. Puree oysters, eggplant, celery and garlic. Make a light roux with flour and butter. Bring oyster liqueur to boil and add roux. Let simmer for 15 minutes. Add cream and simmer for 5 minutes. Add salt and pepper to taste.

Galatoire's Restaurant
Photo by Galatoires.com

Jackson Square Photo © Roy Tennant, FreeLargePhotos.com

Brennan's Restaurant
Photo Brennans.com

Brennan's Restaurant Dining Room
Photo Brennans.com

CHAPTER 2

APPETIZERS

Shrimp Remoulade (From Tujague's)

1 cup ketchup
2 tablespoons horseradish
2 tablespoons yellow mustard
2 teaspoon Worcestershire sauce
Dash Tabasco
4 hard boiled eggs, chopped
2 raw eggs, beaten
1 gallon water
1 package crab boil
3 tablespoons salt
36 large raw shrimp
Shredded lettuce

Mix the first seven ingredients in a glass bowl. Chill in the refrigerator 4 hours. In a large pot, bring the water, crab boil and salt to a full boil. Add shrimp. When the water returns to the boil, turn off the heat and let the shrimp sit for 5 minutes to absorb the seasonings. Drain the shrimp, cool and then peel them. Place 6 shrimp on a plate lined with shredded lettuce and top with 4 tablespoons of the sauce. Repeat 5 more times. Serves 6.

Shrimp Cocktail Sauce For Shrimp, Raw Oysters or Crabmeat (From P & J Oyster Company)

Cocktail Sauce

Ingredients
3/4 cup Tomato Catsup
1 lemon (squeezed
4 Tsp. horseradish
2 Tsp. Worcestershire
1/4 Tsp. Tabasco
1/4 Tsp. onion powder
1/4 Tsp. celery salt

Instructions
Combine all ingredients. Serve with Shrimp, Raw Oysters or Crabmeat

Oyster Patties (P & J Oyster Company)

Ingredients
4 dozen Oysters
dash of cayenne pepper
oyster liqueur from poached oysters
chopped parsley
1 chopped onion
1/4 tsp. of lemon juice
2 tbsp. melted butter or margarine
salt & pepper
1 tbsp. flour
36 small pattie shells
1/2 cup sliced mushrooms

Instructions
Sauté onions, mushrooms, parsley in butter. Blend in flour until smooth. Poach oysters, (about 4 minutes). Add oysters and liqueur, cayenne, lemon juice, salt and pepper to sautéed ingredients and cook on medium-low flame for about 5 minutes. Pour all ingredients into blender and blend until ingredients are smooth. (Blend about 20 seconds.) Pour into pattie shells. Bake at 425 degrees for 10 to 15 minutes.

Shrimp Mold (From Cajun-Recipes.com)

One 10 oz can tomato soup
Three 3 oz pkg cream cheese
1-1/2 envelopes unflavored gelatin
1/4 cup cold water
2 cups (1 lb) boiled shrimp, seasoned and shredded or 3 small cans (4-1/2 oz each) shrimp
1 cup mayonnaise
3/4 cup finely chopped celery
1 small onion, chopped fine
1/4 cup finely chopped green onion tops
Salt, pepper and hot sauce - to taste.

Heat soup and dissolve cheese in it. Continue heating until melted. Remove from heat. Dissolve gelatin in cold water and add to soup mixture. Cool for a while and add all remaining ingredients. Pour into a lightly greased (butter or cooking spray) 6 cup mold. Chill overnight. Serve with crackers.

Ecstasy (From Uglesich's Restaurant)

Makes 2 servings

1 cup crumbled Danish blue cheese
2/3 cup extra-virgin olive oil
2 teaspoons fresh lemon juice
3/4 cup heavy cream
3 tablespoons minced garlic
1/2 cup chopped parsley
1/4 cup medium-dry sherry
2 to 4 tablespoons hot sauce
2 tablespoons fresh lime juice
8 medium shrimp with tails, peeled and deveined
Lettuce

Puree blue cheese, 1/3 cup oil, lemon juice and cream in a food processor until smooth. Transfer to a serving cup.
Place garlic, parsley, 1/3 cup oil, sherry, hot sauce and lime juice in a bowl and stir. Pour some of the sauce into a skillet and set on medium heat.
Place the shrimp in the skillet. Saute until the shrimp turn pink on both sides. Place the shrimp on top of the lettuce on a plate. Put the cup of blue cheese dip on the side.

Marinated crab claws (Posted by The Times-Picayune February 06, 2008 2:44PM)

Crab claws are favorites in many local restaurants, but they're simple to make at home.
Marinated crab claws
Makes 10 to 12 appetizer servings
1 pound shelled crab claws
1/3 cup fresh lime or lemon juice
1 ½ teaspoons salt
½ teaspoon onion powder
¼ cup red wine vinegar
½ cup olive oil
1 tablespoon Worcestershire sauce

Louisiana hot sauce or ground cayenne pepper to taste
¼ teaspoon garlic powderPlace crab claws in a glass or plastic dish. In a small bowl, mix the remaining ingredients together, then pour over the crab claws, cover with a lid or foil and refrigerate overnight, stirring several times.

French-Fried Crab Claws (From Chef John Folse)

PREP TIME: 30 Minutes
SERVES: 6
COMMENT:
Home-style frying units, such as Fry Daddy or Fry Baby, make deep frying simple for the home kitchen. Also be aware of the nice "lite" frying oils available on the market today. Using these will make deep frying a lot healthier.

INGREDIENTS FOR BATTER:
* 1 cup milk
* ½ cup water
* 2 eggs
* 3 tbsps Creole mustard
* salt and cracked black pepper to taste

METHOD:
In a 1-quart mixing bowl, combine all of the above ingredients. Whisk with a wire whip to ensure mixture is well blended. Set aside.

INGREDIENTS FOR BREADING:
2 cups yellow corn flour
2¼ tsps salt
1½ tsps granulated garlic
1½ tsps cracked black pepper
1½ tsps cayenne pepper
1½ tsps dried thyme

METHOD:
In a 1-quart mixing bowl, combine all of the above ingredients. Set aside.

INGREDIENTS FOR FRYING:
1 pound cleaned crab claws
1½ quarts vegetable oil

METHOD:
In a home-style deep fryer, such as a Fry Daddy or Fry Baby, preheat oil according to manufacturer's directions or to 375° F. Place crab claws in batter mixture and allow to sit 10-15 minutes. Drain all excess liquid from crab claws and bread well in yellow corn flour. Shake off all excess breading and deep fry a few dozen at a time until claws turn golden brown and float to top of frying unit. Remove and drain on paper towels and serve hot with cocktail or tartar sauce.
Note: Plain flour can be substituted.

Crab-Stuffed Artichoke Bottoms (From Chef John Folse)

Prep Time: 1 Hour
Yields: 6 Servings
Comment:
One of the most famous soups in South Louisiana is crab and artichoke bisque. The flavors of these two ingredients are often married in Louisiana cuisine. Here is just another example of the flavor of crab and spinach used together to create a delicious appetizer. You may wish to try using oysters instead of crabmeat. Replace the ½ pound of lump crabmeat with 1 cup of oysters.

Ingredients:
12 artichoke bottoms, fresh or canned
½ pound lump crabmeat
¼ cup butter
¼ cup minced onions
¼ cup minced celery
¼ cup minced red bell peppers
1 tbsp minced garlic
2 cups cooked spinach
¼ cup tomato ketchup
salt and cracked pepper to taste
Louisiana hot sauce to taste
½ ounce Herbsaint
½ cup seasoned Italian breadcrumbs
¼ pound butter, melted
1 ounce sherry
2 tbsps chopped parsley

Method:
Preheat oven to 350°F. If the artichoke bottoms are canned, soak in cold water for one hour to remove the brine and vinegar taste. In a heavy-bottomed skillet, melt ¼ cup butter over medium-high heat. Add onions, celery, bell peppers and garlic. Sauté 3-5 minutes or until vegetables are wilted. Chop the cooked spinach very fine and add to the vegetables. Blend well and add lump crabmeat. Stir until all ingredients are well incorporated. Simmer 5 minutes then add ketchup, salt, pepper and hot sauce. Lower heat to simmer and cook 10-15 additional minutes. Add Herbsaint, blend into the crab and spinach mixture and remove from heat. Sprinkle in breadcrumbs and allow the mixture to cool slightly. Once cooled, stuff the center of each artichoke bottom with the crab and spinach mixture. Place the artichokes in a large baking pan and top with an equal portion of melted butter and sherry. Sprinkle with parsley and bake uncovered for 15-20 minutes. Serve 2 artichokes with a spoon of sherry-butter sauce. You may wish to place one whole oyster on the bottom of the artichoke prior to stuffing with the crab and spinach mixture.

Lump Crab and Artichoke Dip (From Chef John Folse)

PREP TIME: 30 Minutes
SERVES: 10 - 12

COMMENT:
For your next cocktail party, especially around the holiday season, no combination is better for a unique and tasty dip than crabmeat and artichokes. An interesting thing about this recipe is the many variations that may come about by simply adding more cream to create a soup or throwing in 2 cups of chopped spinach and replacing the crab meat with oysters for a fabulous Oysters Rockefeller Dip.

Ingredients:

1 pound jumbo lump crabmeat
2 (8½-ounce) cans artichoke hearts, drained
¼ pound butter
½ cup diced onion
¼ cup diced celery
¼ cup diced red bell pepper
¼ cup diced yellow bell pepper
2 tbsps minced garlic
¼ tsp granulated garlic
¼ tsp nutmeg
½ cup flour
2 cups chicken stock
1 pint heavy whipping cream 1 ounce dry white wine
¼ cup sliced green onions
¼ cup chopped parsley
2 cups grated Parmesan cheese
½ tsp salt
¼ tsp cayenne pepper
½ tsp chopped basil

METHOD:
Begin by rinsing artichokes well under cold water to remove the brine. Chop artichokes coarsely in a food processor, remove and set aside for later use. In a 2-quart heavy-bottomed sauté pan, melt butter over medium-high heat. Add onion, celery, bell pepper and garlic. Sauté 3-5 minutes or until vegetables are wilted. Add artichokes and blend well into the vegetable mixture, stir and cook 5 additional minutes. Sprinkle in flour and blend well to form a white roux. Do not brown. Add chicken stock and heavy whipping cream, one cup at a time, whisking constantly until a thick cream sauce is achieved. Reduce heat to simmer. Add >

white wine and season to taste using salt and pepper. Simmer approximately 15 minutes, stirring> occasionally to keep from scorching. The mixture should resemble a thick cream sauce. Should it become too thick, additional whipping cream or stock may be added to reach desired consistency. Add green onions and parsley, then fold in lump crabmeat. Cook 5 minutes longer and remove from heat. Fold in Parmesan cheese and adjust seasonings if necessary. Place the mixture in a chafing dish and serve with garlic croutons or crackers.

Crawfish and Green Onion Sausage Cabbage Rolls (Chef John Folse)

Prep Time: 1 Hour
Yield: 1 Dozen
Comment:
The luck of the Irish smiles upon us, as crawfish are abundant on St. Patrick's Day. This non-traditional cabbage roll combines the flavors of Louisiana with cabbage, which is thrown from St. Patrick's Day parade floats of New Orleans.
Ingredients:
* ½ pound crawfish tails, chopped
* ½ pound fresh green onion sausage, removed from casings
* 12 cabbage leaves blanched
* 2 tsps unsalted butter
* 1 cup diced yellow onions
* ½ cup diced bell peppers
* 1 tsp Creole seasoning
* 1 tbsp minced garlic
* 1 cup cooked white rice
* 1 (8-ounce) can tomato sauce
* salt to taste
* black pepper to taste
* 2 tbsps chopped parsley
* 1 tbsp chopped fresh oregano

Method:
Blanche cabbage leaves by placing leaves in salted boiling water. Boil until soft and pliable. Remove from boiling water and immediately immerse in ice water to stop the cooking process. Remove and pat dry. In a medium skillet, melt butter over medium-high heat. Add onions, bell peppers and Creole seasoning. Cook 5-7 minutes or until wilted an starting to brown. Add garlic and cook 1 minute. Stir in green onion sausage and cook 5- minutes or until no longer pink. Mix in rice, tomato sauce and crawfish then season to taste with salt and pepper. Remove from heat and stir in parsley and oregano. Adjust seasonings if necessary and allow mixture to cool.
Lay cabbage leaves, rib side down, on a flat work surface. Spoon about 3 tablespoons of filling into center of each leaf. Roll each leaf into a neat cylinder, tucking in the sides. Placerolls in the top of a steamer basket. Cover and steam 15-20 minutes then remove basket from the heat. Serve hot on your favorite spaghetti sauce.

CAJUN SPICY SHRIMP & AVOCADO DIP (From Chef John Folse)

Prep Time: 20 Minutes
Yields: 5 Cups

Comment:
This spicy, Mexican-style dip is a twist on the original guacamole. By adding boiled shrimp, the dish is "Cajunized" and is a perfect party food. For extra kick, use hot salsa rather than mild.

Ingredients:
½ pound medium boiled shrimp
2 avocados, diced
½ cup diced onions
1 cup crushed tomatoes
1 tbsp minced garlic
2 tbsps chopped cilantro
3 tbsps fresh lime juice
½ cup tomato sauce
1 (24-ounce) jar salsa
1 tbsp jalapeño peppers, seeded and minced
½ tsp chipotle chili powder
salt to taste

Method:
Peel, devein and coarsely chop shrimp. In a medium bowl, stir all ingredients together until well blended. Serve with your favorite chips.

Crabmeat Au Gratin (From Chef John Folse)

PREP TIME: 45 Minutes
SERVES: 4-6

COMMENT:
Au Gratin refers to the crusty topping that appears on the top of a cheese dish after it is removed from the oven or broiler. The most famous of all Au Gratins in Louisiana is the jumbo lump crabmeat Au Gratin. Try substituting shrimp or even crawfish into the recipe.

INGREDIENTS:

1 pound jumbo lump crabmeat
1/4 pound butter
1 cup celery, chopped
1 cup onion, chopped
1/2 cup red bell pepper, chopped
1 tbsp minced garlic
1/2 tsp flour
1 (13-ounce) can evaporated milk
2 egg yolks
1 tsp salt
1/2 tsp cayenne
1/4 tsp black pepper
1 tbsp basil, chopped
1 tsp thyme, chopped
1/2 pound sharp Cheddar cheese, grated

METHOD:
Preheat oven to 350 degrees F. In a heavy-bottomed sauté pan, melt butter over medium-high heat. Add celery, onion, bell peppers and garlic. Sauté until vegetables are wilted, approximately 3-5 minutes. While vegetables are sautéing, whip egg yolks and evaporated milk until well blended and set aside. Sprinkle flour over seasoning mixture and blend well into the sauté pan to create a white roux. Do Not Brown. Using a wire whisk, add milk/egg mixture while stirring constantly to blend into roux mixture. Season to taste using salt, peppers, basil and thyme. Continue to blend, cooking 3-5 additional minutes. Remove from heat and fold 1/4 pound Cheddar cheese into the white sauce mixture and blend until cheese is totally melted. Place cleaned crabmeat into a Pyrex baking dish. Top with the cheese sauce, then sprinkle with remaining grated cheddar. Cover and bake until bubbly. Uncover then slightly brown the top of the casserole.

Crawfish or Shrimp Cocktail (From Justin Wilson)

For the sauce:

½ cup picante sauce
1 cup catsup
½ cup horseradish sauce
½ teaspoon salt
1 tablespoon fresh lemon or lime juice
½ cup finely chopped fresh parsley
Cayenne pepper to taste
8 to 10 pounds peeled boiled crawfish or shrimp

Combine all the sauce ingredients. Pour over the crawfish or shrimp or dip them in it.

Catfish And Crawfish Mold - Justin Wilson

Ingredients

1 Cup Chopped parsley
1 Cup Cream cheese
1/2 Cup Dry white wine
Salt, to taste
1 Tablespoon Lemon juice
1 Pound Catfish meat, cooked
1 Teaspoon Louisiana hot sauce
1 Pound Crawfish meat, cooked
1 Tablespoon Lea & Perrins

Preparation

Chop catfish and crawfish in food processor.
Add wine, parsley, lemon juice, and salt. Mix real well.
Add hot sauce and Lea & Perrins Worcestershire sauce. Mix well.
Add cream cheese. Mix well.
Refrigerate overnight in a mold.
Serve with crackers or on a bed of lettuce.
You can use shrimp if crawfish aren't available.

Pick Up Sticks (From K-Paul's)
Makes About 32 Springrolls
Ingredients
2 teaspoons Cajun Seasoning (used in place of salt, pepper & other seasonings)
1 teaspoon ground ginger
1/2 teaspoon yellow mustard seeds, whole
1/2 teaspoon ground dried Anaheim chile peppers
1/2 teaspoon ground dried Ancho chile peppers
1/2 teaspoon ground dried New Mexico chile peppers
1/4 cup vegetable oil
1 1/2 cup finely chopped onions
1 cup finely chopped carrots
3/4 cup finely chopped celery
1/2 pound minced pork
1/4 cup mirin (Japanese rice wine)
2 tablespoons soy sauce
2 tablespoons oyster sauce
1 tablespoon minced ginger
1 tablespoon minced garlic
2 teaspoons white sugar
12 ounces finely chopped shrimp
3 tablespoons all purpose flour
1/2 cup finely chopped green onions
1 tablespoon toasted sesame oil
32 lumpia wrappers or springroll wrappers (about 10-inch diameter)
1 egg white, lightly beaten
1/4 cup black sesame seeds
1/4 cup white sesame seeds
vegetable oil, for frying
how to prepare

Combine the first six ingredients in a small bowl to make the Seasoning Mix and set aside.

Heat the oil in a large skillet over high heat, about 2 minutes. Add the onions, carrots and celery and stir well. Cook, stirring frequently, until onions are translucent, about 3 minutes. Add the pork and Seasoning Mix. Cook, stirring frequently and breaking up the meat until the pork is no longer pink, about 3 minutes. Add the mirin, soy sauce, oyster sauce, ginger, garlic and sugar. Stir well until combined, then add the shrimp. Continue to cook and stir until shrimp are half cooked, about 2 minutes. Add the flour and stir in until dissolved. Add the green onions and sesame oil. Stir until evenly mixed, then remove from heat. Spread the mixture in a thin layer on a sheet pan and refrigerate until cold. >

ASSEMBLY

Spread a ½-inch diameter line of filling onto one lumpia/springroll wrapper. Start rolling the wrapper tightly into a cylinder about 3/8-inch diameter. If the wrapper is large, cut off the excess and discard. Seal the edge of the roll with egg white. Brush the outside of the roll lightly with egg white. Sprinkle the outside of the roll lightly with black and white sesame seeds.

In a deep fryer (or in a skillet with 1-inch of oil), fry the springroll in 350°F oil until golden brown and cooked through, 3 to 4 minutes. Serve with Teriyaki Dipping Sauce (recipe follows).

Fried Crawfish (From Alex Patout's)

Ingredients:
3 eggs
2 teaspoon ground black pepper
12 ounces beer (not too dark)
2 teaspoons ground white pepper
2 cups milk
Oil for deep-frying
2 cups all-purpose flour
2 pounds peeled crawfish tails
2 tablespoons salt
1 teaspoon ground red pepper

Instructions:
In a large bowl, beat together the eggs, beer, and milk. Place the flour in a wide shallow bowl. Mix together the salt and peppers and stir half into each bowl. Heat at least 3 inches of oil to 375 degrees F in a deep fryer or large haevy pot.

Pour the crawfish into the beer batter and mix well to coat. Remove about a quarter of the crawfish from the batter, using a slotted spoon to allow the excess batter to drain off, and dredge them in the flour mixture.

Place them in a frying basket and shake the basket to knock off most, but not all, of the excess flour - a little extra is necessary to help the crawfish "bloom" as they fry. Fry the crawfish until they are firm and golden brown, 2-3 minutes. Drain on paper towels. Repeat.
Serves: Serves 8-10 as a first course, 4-6 as main course

Additional Notes:
These delectable little creatures can be served as an appetizer or entree, or any other way your heart desires.

Cajun Stuffed Mushrooms (From Alex Patout's)

Ingredients:
24 large, fresh mushrooms
2 cups plain bread crumbs
2 medium onions chopped fine
2 tablespoons plus a dash of Worchestershire sauce
2 medium bell peppers chopped fine
2 tablespoons plus a dash Tabasco
2 celery ribs chopped fine
2 tablespoons salt
1 pound butter, 3 teaspoons ground red pepper
2 pounds white crabmeat
1/2 cup plus 6 tablespoons fresh lemon juice
2 teaspoons black pepper
1/2 cup plus 4 tablespoons green onions chopped
2 teaspoons white pepper
1/2 cup plus 4 tablespoons parsley chopped
4 tablespoons dry vermouth

Instructions:
Remove the stems from the mushrooms and reserve them for another use (a good Cajun never throws anything away!). Wipe the caps. Saute the onion, bell pepper and celery in 1/2 pound of butter until soft. Stir in the crabmeat and 1/2 cup of the fresh lemon juice and simmer for 10 minutes. Add 4 tablespoons each of the green onions and parsley, all the bread crumbs, and a dash each of Worchestershire and Tabasco sauce. Simmer 4-5 minutes more, stirring often. Season with salt and pepper to taste. Remove dressing from heat and let cool.

Stuff the mushroom caps generously with the dressing and place in a single layer in a shallow ovenproof dish. Melt the remaining 1/2 pound butter and add the remaining 6 tablespoons of lemon juice and 2 tablespoons each of Worchestershire and Tabasco sauce, and the vermouth. Simmer together for 1 minute, pour over the mushrooms, and bake in a preheated 350 degree F oven for 15 minutes, or broil at 450 degree F for 5 minutes.

Serves: Serves 8 as a first course.

Crabmeat Prentiss (From Arnaud's)
Serves 8

Named for Susan and Bill Prentiss, this specialty may also be offered as a a dip served with croutons or crackers.

1/4 cup unsalted butter
1 cup finely chopped onion
1/2 cup finely chopped celery
1/2 cup finely chopped green bell pepper
1 small clove garlic, very finely chopped
1 pound cream cheese, at room temperature
1 cup sour cream
1 pound jumbo lump crabmeat, picked over and all bits of shell and cartilage removed
2 teaspoons Creole seasoning spice mix such as Tony Chachere's or Chef Paul's
2 green onions, white and green parts, thinly sliced
1/4 cup finely chopped fresh parsley
1/2 cup grated Parmesan cheese
1 cup grated Swiss cheese
Parsley sprigs, for garnish

Preheat the oven to 350°. To make the croutons, slice the baguette into 1/4-inch rounds. Arrange the slices on a baking sheet and toast just until pale golden. Turn and brush the other side lightly with olive oil, toast again until golden and set aside.

In a large saucepan, melt the butter over medium-low heat. Add and sauté the onion, celery and bell pepper until translucent, about 7 minutes. Add the garlic and cook for a minute or two, until tender but not browned. Add the cream cheese and sour cream and stir constantly until the cream cheese melts and the mixture comes to a simmer. Gently stir in the crabmeat, reduce the heat to very low and simmer for 3 minutes.

Add the Creole seasoning, green onions, parsley, Parmesan and Swiss cheese. Stir together to blend and bring just to a boil, then remove from the heat.

Divide the mixture among individual ramekins or shallow serving dishes and place on a plate with several croutons alongside each one, for scooping. Garnish with the parsley sprigs and serve hot.

CRABCAKES (From Muriel's)

5 OZ. yellow onion, diced small
4 oz. green bell pepper, diced small
1-1/2 oz. celery, diced small
½ oz. garlic, chopped
1 lb. jumbo lump crabmeat, picked
1 cup creole aioli
4 oz. bread crumbs

Method
Sauté onion, bell pepper, celery and garlic until softened. Cool on a sheet pan. Combine all ingredients and form into 3 ½ oz. crabcakes

Oysters Joseph (From P & J Oyster House)

Ingredients
1 pint Oysters
1 stick butter or margarine
3 toes garlic
1 & 1/2 cups Italian bread crumbs
3 green onions
1/2 cup fresh grated romano cheese
1 lemon

Instructions
Chop garlic and green onions. Sauté onions and garlic in butter in sauté pan. Add oysters. Cook oysters in sauté ed ingredients until oyster mantles curl, (about 2 minutes). Put a layer of bread crumbs on the bottom of a Pyrex pie dish. Pour oysters and sauté ed ingredients on top of the layer of bread crumbs in Pyrex pie dish. Pour rest of bread crumbs on top. Put a layer of romano cheese on top. Broil until cheese is golden brown, (1-2 minutes). Squeeze lemon on top before serving. Serves 4 as an entree or 6 as an appetizer. You can increase servings by increasing ingredients.

Oysters En Brochette (From P & J Oyster Company)

Ingredients
1 Pint of Oysters
1 egg
1 cup of flour
1/2 cup Creole mustard
2 tsp. K-Paul's Seafood Magic
1/2 cup sour cream
12 slices of bacon
1/2 cup real mayonnaise

Instructions
Fry bacon until partially cooked. Bacon has to wrap around oysters so do not overcook. Season flour with seafood magic. Wrap oysters with bacon and skewer with a tooth pick, dip in egg wash, then dip in flour mixture, then dip once again in egg wash, then dip once again in flour mixture. Season again with seafood magic. Fry until crisp.

La Louisiane Restaurant
Photo LaLouisiane.com

Court Of Two Sisters Restaurant
Photo CourtOfTwoSisters.com

Natches Steamboat
Photo © Roy Tennant, FreeLargePhotos.com

CHAPTER 3

SALADS

Crawfish Carboneaux (From Lafitte's Landing)

PREP TIME: 45 Minutes
SERVES: 4 - 6

COMMENT:
This pasta dish was first introduced at Lafitte's Landing Restaurant in 1981. Pasta was coming of age in American cooking and South Louisiana had the perfect ingredients for such a dish. Today, this dish is found throughout America.

INGREDIENTS:

* 3 cups cooked angel hair pasta
* 1 cup cooked crawfish tails
* 1/4 pound butter
* 1 ounce dry white wine
* 1 tbsp chopped garlic
* 1 tbsp lemon juice
* 1/4 cup chopped green onions
* 2 cups heavy whipping cream
* 1/4 cup sliced mushrooms
* 1/4 cup diced red bell pepper
* 1/2 cup diced tomatoes
* 1 tbsp chopped parsley
* 1/2 cup diced andouille or bacon
* salt and cracked black pepper to taste

METHOD:
In a two quart heavy bottom sauce pan, melt butter over medium high heat. Add garlic, green onions, mushrooms, tomatoes and andouille. Saute three to five minutes or until all vegetables are wilted. Add crawfish and cook for an additional two minutes. Deglaze pan with white wine and lemon juice, and continue cooking until volume of liquid is reduced to one half. Add heavy whipping cream and, stirring constantly, reduce until cream is thick and of a sauce-like consistency, approximately five minutes. Add diced red bell pepper and cook for one minute. Remove from heat, add parsley and season to taste using salt and pepper. Gently fold in cooked angel hair pasta and serve. May be chilled and served as a cold pasta salad.

Layered Fruit & Shrimp Salad (From Chef John Folse)

PREP TIME: 1 Hour
SERVES: 10

COMMENT:
Fruit is not just for dessert anymore! With its wide range of colors and textures, nothing makes a more beautiful entrée salad than layers of fresh or canned fruit. Why not create an interesting and unique summer salad by combining colorful, healthful fruit with fresh shrimp or other seafood?

INGREDIENTS:

- 2 cups watermelon balls
- 2 cups cantaloupe balls
- 2 cups honeydew balls
- 2 cups sliced peaches
- 2 cups sliced pears
- 2 cups quartered orange sections
- 2 cups sliced plums
- 1 cup fresh blueberries
- 1 cup fresh strawberries
- 1 cup cubed pineapple
- 2 dozen (21-25) count boiled shrimp
- 2 cups crawfish tails
- 1 recipe fruity yogurt dressing
- ½ cup chopped pecans

METHOD:
In a large glass serving bowl, layer fruit by alternating stratas of color. Once all the fruit has been layered, line shrimp and crawfish in a decorative pattern around the edge of the bowl. Top with fruity yogurt dressing, and toss the mixture to blend the dressing into the fruit. Sprinkle with pecans and serve immediately.

Marinated Crawfish, Zucchini and Summer Squash Salad (From Chef John Folse)

PREP TIME: 1 Hour
SERVES: 6

COMMENT:
Romantics say that it's the simple things in life that are best. Well if that's so, then this simple crawfish and squash salad should set hearts aglow. I recommend serving it in a beautiful cut crystal bowl to enhance its presentation.

INGREDIENTS:

* 1 pound crawfish tails
* 3 medium zucchini squash, shredded
* 3 medium summer squash, shredded
* 1 small Bermuda onion, thinly sliced
* 1/2 red bell pepper, julienned
* 1/2 yellow bell pepper, julienned
* 2 tbsps garlic, minced
* 1/4 cup sweet pickle relish
* 1/3 cup salad oil
* 1/3 cup red wine vinegar
* 1 tsp dried basil
* 1 tsp dried thyme
* 1 tsp salt
* 1 tsp cracked black pepper

METHOD:
In a large mixing bowl, combine crawfish, squash, 1 small Bermuda onion, bell peppers, garlic and relish. In a separate mixing bowl, combine salad oil, wine vinegar, basil, thyme, salt and pepper. Using a wire whisk, whip until well-blended. Pour marinade evenly over vegetable mixture, cover and refrigerate salad overnight. Prior to serving, toss and drain off any excess liquid. Place the salad into a decorative serving bowl and garnish with edible flower petals such as pansies, dianthus, violets or marigolds.

Shrimp and Avocado Salad with Orange Vinaigrette (From Chef John Folse)

Yields: 4 Servings
Prep Time: 30 Minutes

Ingredients for Vinaigrette:

* ¼ cup fresh orange juice
* 2 tsps fresh lime juice
* 2 tsps minced shallots
* 2 tsps Creole mustard
* 1 tsp chopped parsley
* ½ tsp chopped orange zest
* 1 tbsp sugar
* 1/8 tsp cayenne pepper
* ½ cup olive oil
* salt and cracked black pepper to taste

Method:
In a blender, combine orange juice, lime juice, shallots, mustard, parsley, zest, sugar and cayenne pepper. Blend on medium speed 2 minutes until puréed and emulsified. While blender is running, slowly add olive oil until combined. Add salt and pepper to taste. Blend until seasonings are well incorporated. Set dressing aside.

Ingredients for Salad:

* ½ pound large shrimp, peeled, tail intact
* 2 avocados
* 2 oranges
* 1 tbsp fresh lime juice
* 2 tbsps olive oil
* salt and black pepper to taste
* Zatarain's Creole seasoning to taste
* ½ tsp granulated garlic
* ¼ cup chopped pecans
* 2 tsps fresh chopped tarragon
* 2 cups baby spinach
* 2 radishes thinly sliced

Method:
With a sharp paring knife, peel oranges and remove all white pith. Cut orange segments free from membranes. Quarter avocados lengthwise, then pit and peel. Cut lengthwise into ¼-inch slices. Drizzle with lime juice and season with salt and pepper. Heat oil in a skillet over high heat until hot but not smoking. Pat shrimp >

dry and season with salt, pepper, Creole seasoning and granulated garlic. Sauté shrimp turning them until just cooked through. Add pecans and tarragon. Toss well. Sauté for 1 minute longer. In a salad bowl, toss spinach, half of orange segments and radishes with half of vinaigrette. Arrange avocados and remaining orange segments on 4 plates and top with salad and shrimp. Spoon the remaining vinaigrette over salad and serve.

Paneed Oyster Salad with Creole Mustard Dressing (From P & J Oyster Company)

Serves 6-8.

Ingredients
1 pint oysters
2 cups Italian Bread Crumbs
3 eggs
2 heads Bibb lettuce
1 Tbsp. Creole mustard
4 Tbsp. Olive oil
1 Tsp. red wine vinegar
Salt and pepper
2 cups vegetable oil
Romano cheese

Instructions
Separate egg yolks and save egg whites. To make dressing, mix egg yolks, Creole mustard, Olive oil, vinegar and salt and pepper to taste. Put oysters in egg whites. Batter oysters with bread crumbs. Fry battered oysters in vegetable oil until golden brown. Place cleaned lettuce leave on plates and sprinkle with romano cheese. Place 4 oysters on lettuce. Pour dressing over oysters and lettuce.

JUMBO SHRIMP SALAD WITH CREOLE CREAM CHEESE DRESSING (From Chef: Bittersweet Plantation)

Ingredients:
2 dozen 21-25 count Louisiana shrimp, peel & deveined
1 container Chef John Folse's Bittersweet Plantation Dairy Creole Cream Cheese
2 cups heavy whipping cream
3/4 tsp. ground nutmeg
3/4 tsp. ground cinnamon
3/4 cup sugar
2 (8oz. cans fruit cocktail, drained very well)
1 cup chopped pecans
2 1/2 cups seedless green grapes
2 cups shredded coconut
2 (11 ounce) cans mandarin oranges, drained
10 ounce jar maraschino cherries, drained
2 (8 ounce) cans pineapple chunks, drained

It is important to drain the fruit very well so that there will be no excess moisture in the finished dessert. In a large pot, salt water and boil shrimp until just done, about 2-4 minutes. Set aside to cool. In the bowl of a mixer, combine Creole cream cheese, whipping cream, nutmeg and cinnamon. Whip on medium high speed. When mixture starts to thicken slightly, add sugar slowly and beat until stiff peaks form. Set aside. When layering the whipped cream between fruit, use a generous amount. In a glass trifle bowl, layer in order: fruit cocktail, whipped cream, pecans, whipped cream, grapes, coconut, mandarin oranges, whipped cream, 16 shrimp, marshmallows, cherries, whipped cream and pineapple. Top with remaining whipped cream. Garnish with mint and maraschino cherries and place 8 jumbo shrimp curled over the edges of the bowl. This recipe can be created in individual servings by layering the ingredients in the same manner in parfait or pilsner glasses.

Boiled Shrimp Salad (From LouisianaFishFry.com)

Makes 2 large salads
INGREDIENTS:
* 1 lb unpeeled shrimp
* 1 bottle shrimp and crab boil
* 1 tomato cut into chuncks
* 1/2 head iceberg lettuce chopped
* 1 bottle Louisiana Fish Fry Products Remoulade Dressing
* 2 hardboiled eggs
* Green onions chopped for garnish

DIRECTIONS:
1. Boil shrimp according to directions on shrimp and crab boil bottle.
2. Once cooled, peel shrimp
3. Assemble lettuce, tomato and egg on salad plates
4. Top with shrimp and green onions
5. Serve with Remoulade Dressing.

Fried Crawfish Salad (From Zatarain's)

Fried crawfish tails are crunchy and delicious. They are doubly tasty when served over salad greens drizzled with Zatarain's® Creole Mustard Honey Vinaigrette.

Makes 4 servings.
Prep Time: 15 minutes, Cook Time: 10 minutes
Ingredients:
Vegetable oil for frying
1/2 cup Zatarain's® Crispy Southern Style Seasoned Fish-Fri®
1/2 pound shelled crawfish tails
8 cups salad greens
1 tomato, sliced
1/2 cup Zatarain's® Creole Mustard Honey Vinaigrette (recipe link below)

Directions:
1. Pour oil into deep heavy skillet, filliing no more than 1/3 full. Heat on medium-high heat to 350°F.
2. Place Fish-Fri in shallow dish. Coat crawfish in Fish-Fri, a handful at a time; shake off excess. Fry in batches in hot oil 1 1/2 to 2 minutes or until golden brown. Drain on paper towels.
3. Divide salad greens and tomato slices among 4 serving plates. Drizzle each with 2 tablespoons of the Zatarain's® Creole Mustard Honey Vinaigrette. Top with crawfish. Serve immediately.

Fried Crawfish Tails with Olive Salad (From Emeril's)

Ingredients

- 2 pounds crawfish tails
- 1/2 cup buttermilk
- Cajun Seasoning
- 1 cup masa flour
- 1 cup flour
- 1 cup black olives, pitted and quartered
- 1 cup queen stuffed olives, quartered
- 2 tablespoons minced shallots
- 2 teaspoons minced garlic
- 2 tablespoons small diced celery
- 2 tablespoons chopped parsley
- 1 1/2 teaspoons fine ground black pepper
- 1/2 cup olive oil
- 1 cup Lemon Butter Sauce, recipe follows
- Garnish: 1/4 cup grated Parmigiano-Reggiano cheese and parsley leaves

Directions

In a mixing bowl, marinate the crawfish in the buttermilk. Season with Cajun Seasoning, allow to sit for 20 minutes. In a mixing bowl, combine the masa and flour together. Season with Cajun Seasoning. For olive salad, in a mixing bowl, combine the remaining ingredients together and set aside. Dredge the marinated crawfish in the flour mixture and sift to remove any excess. Fry until golden, about 2 to 3 minutes. Stir constantly to prevent from sticking together. Remove from the fryer and drain on paper towels. Season with Essence. To serve, spoon the sauce in the center of each plate. Mound the crawfish in the center of each plate. Spoon the olive salad over the crawfish. Garnish with cheese and parsley.

Bourbon Street Scene
Photo © Roy Tennant, FreeLargePhotos.com

Carriage Ride in front of the Cornstalk Fence Hotel
Photo © Roy Tennant, FreeLargePhotos.com

CHAPTER 4

SIDE DISHES

**Hush Puppies
Commander's Palace, New Orleans**

1 cup yellow cornmeal
1 cup flour
1 tablespoon baking powder
1 teaspoon salt
Pinch of cayenne
Dash of Worcestershire
Freshly ground black pepper
1 cup chilled milk
2 eggs
1/2 teaspoon Tabasco
1/4 cup chopped scallions
2 tablespoons minced shallots or onion
1 garlic clove, minced

Combine cornmeal, flour, baking powder, salt, cayenne, Worcestershire and black pepper in large bowl. Add milk, eggs and Tabasco and stir with fork until blended. Mix in scallions, shallots and garlic. Let stand 30 minutes. Heat oil in deep fryer to 350 degrees F. Drop batter by tablespoonfuls into oil (in batches, do not crowd) and fry until golden brown, about 3 minutes. Remove using slotted spoon and drain on paper towels.

Cajun Eggplant Dressing (From Alex Patout's)

Ingredients:
2 pounds medium shrimp- heads off, 4-6 dashes Tabasco sauce, 4 cups water, 1 teaspoon dried thyme or 1 tablespoon fresh, 1/2 pound margarine, 1 teaspoon dried basil or 1 tablespoon fresh, 3 large onions (chopped fine), 2 medium bell peppers (chopped fine), 2 celery ribs (chopped fine), 1/2 teaspoon dried oregano or teaspoons fresh, 4 medium eggplants, 1 pound cooked crabmeat (claw or white), 1-1/2 teaspoons red pepper, 1 cup chopped green onions, 1-1/2 teaspoons white pepper, 1-1/2 teaspoons black pepper, 1 cup chopped parsley, 1-1/2 teaspoons salt, Grated Parmesan cheese, Bread crumbs

Instructions:
Peel and devein the shrimp; set aside. Place the peels in a small saucepan and add the water. Bring to a boil and reduce by half over medium-high heat, 15-20 minutes. Strain and set aside.

Melt the margarine over medium-high heat in a Dutch oven or other large heavy pot and add the onions, peppers, and celery. Cook the vegetables until they are very soft, stirring occasionally, 30-45 minutes.

Meanwhile, peel the eggplants and cut them into 1-inch cubes. Place them in a saucepan and add water to cover. Bring to a boil and boil slowly for a few minutes, just until tender. Drain. Puree until smooth in blender or food processor.

Add the eggplant, shrimp stock, seasonings, and herbs to the vegetable mixture, return to a simmer, and cook over medium heat for 10 minutes, stirring occasionally. Add the shrimp and continue to cook over medium,-high heat just until the shrimp turn pick, 5-7 minutes. Add the crab meat and cook just long enough to heat through. Remove from heat and stir in green onions and parsley. Spoon the hot dressing into a casserole or individual ramekins. Sprinkle generously with Parmesan cheese and bread crumbs and glaze under the broiler for a couple of minutes.

Serves: Serves 6-8.

Crabmeat Stuffing (From Mulate's Cajun Restaurant)

Ingredients:

1 1/2 sticks butter or margarine
2 medium bell peppers - chopped
3 large onions - chopped
3 stalks celery - chopped
1 tsp. salt
1 tsp. cayenne pepper
2 cups bread crumbs
1 tbsp. Flour
3 eggs
1 handful chapped parsley
3/4 - 1 lb. claw crabmeat - (suit to taste)
(Pick all of the shells out.)

Directions:

Melt butter or margarine.
Sauté' vegetables (bell peppers, onions, and celery) on medium heat until translucent - approximately 15 minutes.
Season with salt and cayenne pepper.
Mix all ingredients except crabmeat.
Add vegetable mixture you've already cooked.
Mix well.
Fold in crabmeat.
To Fry:

Batter in egg and mild mixture.
Cover with bread crumbs.
Fry until golden brown.
To Bake:

Heat oven to 350 degrees.
Cook approximately 20 to 30 minutes.

You can use this stuffing in Stuffed Mushrooms, Stuffed Bell Peppers, and Stuffed Crabs

Oyster Dressing

Serves 10-15

Ingredients
2 pints Oysters
1 cup vegetable oil
20 chicken gizzards
3 cups of Italian bread crumbs
5 chopped chicken livers
2 medium onions
1 bunch of celery
1 sweet pepper
15 sprigs of parsley
1 small loaf stale French bread
15 green
salt and pepper
1 turkey gizzard & liver

Instructions
Boil livers and gizzards in 3 cups of water, (KEEP BROTH). Soak French bread and bread crumbs for 10 minutes. Drain excess liquid. Chop celery, onions, green onions, sweet pepper, in food processor or blender. Chop all gizzards and livers in food processor or blender. Poach oysters for 4 minutes. Chop the poached oysters and save oyster liqueur. Simmer, in oil, all chopped vegetables on medium-low heat for 5 minutes. Add drained bread ingredients. Add chopped oysters and oyster liqueur. Add butter, parsley, and broth. Salt and pepper to taste. Simmer on low heat for about 1/2 hour or until the dressing become dry enough for your taste.

Stuffed Potatoes Au Wayne (From Justin Wilson)

6 large potatoes
Chopped green onions
½ lb. butter or oleo
6 tbs. sour cream
2 tsp. black peppers
Cooked shrimp, crab, or crawfish, 2 tbs. per potato, chopped fine
¼ to ½ tsp. ground cayenne pepper
2 tsp. garlic powder

Rub each potato with cooking oil. Bake potatoes 1 hour. Cut the top off lengthwise and scoop out and reserve the middle. Save the potato shells for stuffing.
Mix the rest of the ingredients together with the reserved cooked potato filling. Fill potato shells with stuffing. Sprinkle with cayenne pepper, if desired. Wrap in foil or Plastic Wrap, then heat in microwave, oven or grill until hot.

Okra and Shrimp Maurice (From Justin Wilson)

Maurice is a Mississippi Cajun, and a damned fine cook. He says to eat this like a cochon. That's like a pig.

¼ cup oil

1½ pounds okra, stems cut off and sliced thin

1 large chopped onion

2 large tomatoes, peeled and pureed

4 large cloves garlic, crushed and pureed

1 teaspoon salt

¾ teaspoon ground thyme

Louisiana hot sauce or ground cayenne pepper to taste

1 pound raw shrimp, peeled and deveined

Heat the oil in a large, high-walled skillet over low heat. Simmer the okra, onions, tomatoes, and garlic together 1½ to 2 hours or until the okra cooks apart and the other vegetables come together. Stir often to avoid burning. Add the salt, thyme, hot sauce, and shrimp, and cook until the shrimp turn pink, only a few minutes.

Creole Jambalaya (From Arnaud's)

Jambalaya is a Creole dish that appears often at casual parties and family get-togethers. It is about as versatile as your pantry allows - you can start with all fresh ingredients or use leftovers. We make seafood jambalaya, or sometimes we mix several ingredients, such as shrimp and chicken or sausage, or ham and chicken. Try this version to start, then let your taste buds or the contents of your refrigerator be your guide.

2 pounds jumbo shrimp, peeled and deveined
2 tablespoons vegetable oil
1/2 pound seasoned sausage such as andouille, diced
1/2 cup chopped green onion
2 cloves garlic, chopped
1/4 cup chopped fresh parsley
1 cup chopped green pepper
1-1/2 cups canned tomatoes
1 bay leaf
1 teaspoon crushed thyme
1/8 teaspoon Cayenne pepper
1/2 teaspoon salt
1-1/2 cups broth (preferred) or water
1 cup long grain rice

Prepare shrimp. In a Dutch oven or a heavy pan with a tight-fitting lid, sauté sausage in the oil for about 3 minutes. Add garlic, onion and green pepper. Cook until tender.
Add parsley, tomatoes, seasonings, rice and water. Stir in thoroughly then add shrimp. Bring to a boil, reduce heat and cover tightly. Cook without stirring over low heat, or transfer to 350 degree oven, for 25-30 minutes or until rice is fluffy. Remove bay leaf before serving.

Barbecued Shrimp (From Court Of Two Sisters)

Ingredients:
48 large shrimp, heads on
4 tbs. Ground black pepper
½ tsp. Cayenne pepper
½ lb. melted butter
1-cup water
½ lb. melted butter
(DO NOT add salt)
French Bread

Procedure:
Select 48 (approximately 2 ½ lbs.) 16-20-count shrimp with heads on and place in a shallow baking dish large enough to contain shrimp in a double layer. Add water and one half pound of butter. Sprinkle shrimp with black pepper and cayenne and cover with second half pound of butter. Place in a hot oven (375 to 400 degrees) and roast for ten minutes. Turn with a large spoon and roast for another ten minutes until shrimp are an even robust pink. Serve with extra loaves of French bread to mop up the delicious liquor created by the butter and roasted shrimp. Serves 4.

CRAWFISH OR SHRIMP AND GOAT CHEESE CREPES (From Muriel's)

Sauce
1 OZ. yellow onion, diced
½ oz. bell pepper, diced
1 oz. tomato, diced
¼ t garlic, chopped
1 t Creole seasoning
4 oz. crawfish tails or 50 ct. shrimp
1 oz. white wine
1 oz. unsalted butter
1 t of oil
Salt and pepper to taste

Crepe Stuffing
crepes
3 oz. goat cheese
2 oz. cream cheese
½ t shallot, chopped
½ t chives, chopped
¼ t salt
¼ t pepper
Mix all ingredients together pipe into crepes and roll up

Method
Place oil in sauté pan over medium high heat, add onions and bell pepper, sauté until softened. Add tomato, garlic and creole seasoning. Sauté 30 seconds. Add crawfish or shrimp sauté 30 seconds more, then add the white wine. Reduce slightly then add butter. Salt and pepper to taste, pour over warmed crepes

Oak Alley Plantation near New Orleans
Photo © Roy Tennant, FreeLargePhotos.com

Steamboat and New Orleans Skyline
Photo © Roy Tennant, FreeLargePhotos.com

Swamp Gator in Houma near New Orleans
Photo © Roy Tennant, FreeLargePhotos.com

CHAPTER 5

ENTREES

Oysters Bienville (From Arnaud's)

2/3 cup finely chopped mushrooms
1 teaspoon ground white pepper
4 tablespoons unsalted butter
1/2 cup brandy
1 1/2 teaspoons finely minced garlic
1/2 teaspoon cayenne
1 tablespoons finely chopped shallots
1 teaspoon salt
1/2 cup heavy cream
6 tablespoons grated Romano cheese
1 tablespoon flour
4 tablespoons dry bread crumbs
1/2 pound boiled shrimp, finely diced
1/4 cup parsley, finely diced
2 dozen oysters on the half shell, drained
4 pans rock salt

In a large, heavy saucepan, sauté the 2/3 cup chopped mushrooms quickly in a small amount of vegetable oil. Remove from pan and set aside. In the same pan, melt the 4 tablespoons unsalted butter and render the garlic and shallots, stirring frequently until soft. Add the diced shrimp, then sprinkle in the flour. Stir all together, add the reserved mushrooms. Deglaze pan with the brandy while stirring constantly. Stir in the heavy cream, cook until smooth before adding Romano cheese, dry bread crumbs and parsley, salt, pepper and cayenne. A small amount of milk may be added if the mixture is too thick.

Remove from heat, allow to cool then refrigerate for about 1 1/2 hours. Half an hour before you plan to bake the oysters, place the pans of rock salt in a preheated 500-degree F oven.

Wash oyster shells well, pat dry. Put oysters on shells, place six in each pan of rock salt. Spoon one heaping tablespoon of sauce over each oyster. Bake for 15 to 18 minutes until well browned. Serves 4.

OYSTERS ROCKEFELLER (From Brennan's)

* 1 pound butter
* 1 celery rib, finely chopped
* 2 bunches scallions, finely chopped
* 1 bunch parsley, finely chopped
* 3 tablespoons Worcestershire sauce
* 1 teaspoon Tabasco
* ½ to ¾ cup Herbsaint or Pernod
* 1¼ cups seasoned bread crumbs
* 48 oysters, in their shells
* Rock salt

Melt the butter in a large skillet and add the celery, scallions and parsley. Sauté for 5 minutes, then add the Worcestershire and Tabasco. Reduce heat to medium and cook for 10 minutes. Add the Herbsaint or Pernod and bread crumbs and cook for another 5 minutes. Remove the pan from the heat and transfer the mixture to a bowl. Chill in the refrigerator for 1 hour, until cold but not firmly set.

Using an oyster knife, pry open the oyster shells, then remove the oysters. Discard the top shells; scrub and dry the bottom shells. Drain the oysters. Arrange 6 oyster shells on an ovenproof pan or tray lined with a layer of rock salt about an inch deep. Make 8 trays in all. Place 1 oyster in each shell.

Preheat the oven to 375 degrees F.

Remove the chilled Rockefeller topping from the refrigerator and beat it with an electric mixer to evenly distribute the butter and infuse air into the mixture; transfer the mixture to a pastry bag fitted with a large plain tip. Pipe a tablespoon of the mixture onto each oyster; then bake in the hot oven for 5 to 8 minutes. Serve each person a tray of piping hot oysters.

Makes 8 servings.

Crabmeat Imperial (From Brennan's)

* 1 pound lump crabmeat, picked over to remove any shell and cartilage*
* 1/2 cup scallions, finely chopped
* 1/2 cup green bell pepper, finely chopped
* 1/4 cup chopped pimentos
* 1 egg yolk
* 1 teaspoon dry mustard
* 4 artichoke hearts, coarsely chopped
* 2 tablespoons paprika
* 1 cup mayonnaise
* 1/4 cup freshly grated Parmesan cheese
* 1/4 cup seasoned bread crumbs
* Salt and black pepper

Preheat oven to 375 degrees. In a large bowl, combine the crabmeat, scallions, bell pepper, pimento, egg yolk, dry mustard, artichoke hearts, paprika and one-half cup of the mayonnaise. Stir until well-mixed and season with salt and pepper to taste.

Spoon the crabmeat mixture into four one-cup baking dishes; then cover with the remaining mayonnaise. Sprinkle Parmesan and bread crumbs on top and bake in the hot oven for 15 to 20 minutes until heated through. Serve immediately.

*One pound of blanched crawfish tails can be substituted for the crabmeat. Makes four servings.

Barbecued Shrimp
Emeril's Restaurant

  2 pounds (about 42) medium shrimp
  2 tablespoons Emeril's Creole Seasoning
  scant 1/4 teaspoon freshly ground black pepper
  3 tablespoons olive oil
  1/4 cup chopped onion
  2 tablespoons minced garlic
  3 bay leaves
  3 lemons, peel and pith cut away, flesh halved
  2 cups water
  1/2 cup Worcestershire sauce [or purchased]
  1/4 cup dry white wine
  1/4 teaspoon salt
  2 cups heavy cream
  2 tablespoons unsalted butter, cut into bits
  Fresh chives for garnish

Peel the shrimp, leaving tail and first joint of the shell intact. Reserve shells. Sprinkle shrimp with 1 tablespoon Creole seasoning and half the pepper; rub seasoning in to coat them well. Reserve the shrimp on a baking sheet, chilled and uncovered, to keep them as dry as possible.
In large saucepan heat 1 tablespoon oil over moderately high heat until it is
hot but not smoking. Sauté onion and garlic, stirring, 1 minute. Add reserved shells, remaining 1 tablespoon Creole seasoning, bay leaves, lemons, water, Worcestershire, wine, salt and remaining pepper. Bring mixture to a boil, stirring, and simmer 30 minutes. Let sauce cool 15 minutes, strain it through
a fine sieve into a small saucepan. Boil it 12 to 15 minutes until reduced to about 1/4 cup. In a large skillet heat 1 tablespoon remaining oil over moderately high
heat until hot but not smoking. In it sear half the shrimp, shaking skillet occasionally for 1 minute on each side. Transfer them to a bowl. Heat remaining 1 tablespoon oil and sear remaining shrimp in same manner, transferring them to bowl. Into skillet stir the cream and the sauce, simmer
the barbecue sauce, stirring occasionally, 8 to 10 minutes, or until it is
reduced to about 2 cups. Stir in the shrimp, simmer 1 minute or until
shrimp are heated through; stir in butter. Spoon the sauce onto 4 or 6
heated plates, arrange the shrimp and biscuits (Mini Buttermilk Biscuits)
on the sauce, and garnish each serving with chives.
Serve 6 as a first course or 4 as an entrée.

Shrimp à la Creole (From Corinne Dunbar's)

3 pounds shrimp
1 tablespoon shortening
1 medium sized onion, chopped
2 pieces celery, chopped
1 pod garlic, minced
1 small bell (green) pepper, chopped
1/2 can tomatoes [no size is given, use your judgment]
1/2 can tomato paste [no size is given]
3 sprigs thyme
1 bay leaf
1 tablespoon chopped parsley
1/2 tablespoon sugar
Salt and pepper to taste
Boiled rice

Boil shrimp approximately 10 minutes, peel and clean. Melt shortening in a skillet and add onion, celery, garlic and bell pepper. Simmer 5 minutes and add tomatoes, tomato paste, thyme, bay leaf, parsley, sugar and salt and pepper. Mix well and add shrimp. Simmer 1/2 hour and serve in a circle of boiled rice. Serves 6.

NOTE: These days, the shrimp would not be cooked nearly that long, as they will toughen. Depending on the size of the shrimp, the boiling time might be between 5 and 8 minutes, and the cooked shrimp would be added to the Creole Sauce very shortly before serving.

Seafood Jambalaya (From Commander's Palace)

2 tablespoons butter
1 pound andouille sausage, in 1/4-inch slices
1 large bell pepper, any color, in large dice
3 ribs celery, in large dice
1 small head garlic, cloves peeled and minced
Creole Seafood Seasoning or
any Creole seasoning, to taste
Kosher salt and freshly ground black pepper to taste
2 large tomatoes, cored, peeled, seeded, and chopped
1 pound medium shrimp, peeled
1/2 pound fish fillets, diced
(trout, catfish, redfish, bass, and
bluefish would work well)
2 bay leaves
3 cups long-grain rice, rinsed 3 times
6 cups water
1 pint shucked oysters, with their liquor
2 bunches green onions, thinly sliced
1/4 teaspoon hot sauce, or to taste

Combine the butter and sausage in a Dutch oven or heavy-gauge pot over high heat, and sate for about 6 minutes, stirring occasionally. Add the bell pepper, onion, celery, and garlic, and season with Creole seasoning, salt, and black pepper. Sauté, still over high heat, for about 8 minutes, or until the natural sugars in the vegetables have browned and caramelized.
Add the tomatoes, shrimp, fish, and bay leaves, and stir. Add the rice, stir gently, and add the water. Gently move the spoon across the bottom of the pot, making sure that the rice is not sticking. Bring to a boil, then reduce the heat, cover, and simmer for about 15 minutes or until the rice has absorbed most of the liquid. Turn off the heat, then fold in the oysters, cover, and let sit for about 8 minutes, during which time the jambalaya will continue cooking from residual heat.
To serve, transfer to a serving bowl, and mix in the green onions. Season with hot sauce.
Note: Jambalaya is a very versatile dish, so different combinations of other ingredients will work well in this recipe. If you'd rather use chicken instead of fish, or if you'd prefer to omit the oysters, go ahead.
After adding the rice, the less stirring you do the better. You don't want to pull out excessive starch from the grain. This is not risotto. While simmering, be sure the rice is not sticking to the bottom. If it is, you might need to add a little water or reduce the heat.
If no andouille is available, another smoked sausage may be substituted.

Shrimp and Fettuccine (From Commander's Palace)

4 servings

24 medium shrimp, peeled and deveined,
shells reserved for broth
1/2 cup (1 stick) unsalted butter, softened, divided
2 garlic cloves, minced
4 teaspoons finely chopped parsley
1/2 onion, chopped
4 fresh mushrooms, sliced
1/4 cup peeled, seeded, finely chopped tomato
1/2 cup chopped green onions
2 teaspoons Creole Seafood Seasoning
2 cups cooked fettuccine
1/2 cup dry white wine

Place shrimp shells in a medium saucepan and cover with water. Bring to
a boil; lower heat and simmer 15 minutes. Strain broth and return to saucepan. Boil broth until reduced to 1/4 cup. Set aside.
Melt half the butter in a large saucepan over medium heat. Add the garlic, parsley, onion, mushrooms, tomato, green onions and seafood seasoning; sauté 2 to 3 minutes. Add the broth, cooked fettuccine, shrimp and wine; cook over medium high heat until liquid is almost evaporated. Remove
pan from heat, add remaining butter and stir gently until butter is melted
and sauce creamy. Serve immediately.

Trout Veronique (From The Caribbean Room)

1 trout fillet (from a 1 1/2-pound trout)
1/2 pint [1 cup] white wine
1/2 cup rich Hollandaise sauce
8 seedless grapes

Poach trout in wine in a pan small enough so that wine covers trout. After poaching about 7 minutes, remove trout, draining well, and place on an ovenproof serving plate. Reduce remaining liquid over a fast fire to 2 cooking spoons of liquid. Add Hollandaise sauce and stir briskly. Place grapes on trout, cover with sauce, and glaze quickly in broiler. Serves 1.

Rich Hollandaise Sauce
5 egg yolks
1/4 cup wine tarragon vinegar
Dash Tabasco sauce
4 sticks [1 pound] butter, melted
Salt to taste
1/8 cup tepid water

Combine in a stainless steel mixing bowl the egg yolks, vinegar, and Tabasco sauce. Whip until very frothy, and while continuing to whip, gradually add melted butter (heated to 200 degrees F.) in the manner of making mayonnaise. When butter has been blended, season and add
water to rectify consistency. Makes approximately 3 cups.

Stuffed Flounder (From Brennan's)

Stuffing:
3 tablespoons butter
1/4 cup finely chopped green onions
1/4 cup flour
3/4 cup fish stock
3 tablespoons white wine
1/4 teaspoon salt
Dash cayenne
1 egg yolk, beaten
1/3 cup crab meat
1/2 cup boiled shrimp, peeled and veined
1/2 dozen oysters, lightly blanched
2 teaspoons finely chopped parsley
6 tablespoons paprika
5 tablespoons Parmesan cheese
3 tablespoons bread crumbs
1/4 cup vegetable oil
2 flounders (1 1/2 pounds each)

Over medium heat in 9-inch skillet, melt butter and sauté onions until tender. Blend in the flour thoroughly. Cook slowly about 5 minutes stirring constantly; do not brown. Remove skillet from heat. Blend in fish stock,
wine, salt and pepper, until smooth. Blend in egg yolk thoroughly. Return pan to heat and gently cook over low heat, stirring constantly, about 15 minutes. Add crab meat, shrimp, oysters and parsley and mix thoroughly, heat through and remove from heat.
How to prepare flounder: Cut head from fish, with fish lying flat, dark side up, make a slit from head to tail with boning knife, going through flesh to bone. Now with tail section of fish toward you, take a boning knife and work from center slit to fins loosening the flesh from the bone. Turn fish so that tail is now away from you and insert blade of knife under backbone. Work from center to side in a slicing motion to loosen back of fish from
bone. With a scissors, cut bone loose from fins. Now lift backbone and break away from fish near tail. Your flounder is ready for the stuffing prepared above.
Fill with stuffing and sprinkle with a mixture of 6 tablespoons paprika, 5 tablespoons Parmesan cheese and 3 tablespoons bread crumbs. Close fish.
In a large (12-inch) cast-iron skillet sear flounders in 1/4 cup vegetable oil. Place skillet with flounders into 400-degree F. oven about 20 minutes, or
until done. Serve with lemon slices and parsley. 2 servings.

Cajun Seafood Baked Eggplant (From Emeril's)

1/2 cup (1 stick) butter
1/4 pound hot link sausages, diced
[Cajun andouille would be great!]
1/4 pound chicken gizzards, diced
3 medium eggplants, peeled and diced
3 green bell peppers, seeded and chopped
[We use 1 each green, red and yellow]
3 medium onions, chopped
2 garlic cloves, minced
[or to taste... we use more!]
1 bunch green onions, chopped
1/2 cup chopped celery
1/2 pound small shrimp, shelled, deveined
1 cup cooked rice
1/4 cup fresh parsley, minced
1 teaspoon mixed Italian herbs
1/2 pound lump crabmeat
1/2 cup Italian breadcrumbs
2-3 tablespoons butter
Lemon slices, parsley

Melt 1/2 cup butter in Dutch oven or large saucepan over medium high heat. Add sausage and gizzards and sauté until browned, about 5 minutes. Stir in eggplant, bell pepper, onion, garlic, green onion, and celery. Continue to cook, stirring occasionally, about 15 minutes. Add shrimp, rice, parsley, Italian seasoning and salt. Cook, stirring occasionally, until shrimp is pink and translucent, about 15 minutes. Remove from heat.
Preheat oven to 350 degrees F. Add crabmeat to eggplant mixture with enough breadcrumbs to absorb the remaining butter (may be as little as 1/3 cup). Spoon into individual ramekins. Sprinkle with remaining breadcrumbs and dot with butter. Bake until tops are browned. Garnish with lemon slices and parsley. Serves 8 to 10.

Cajun Seafood Au Gratin (From Alex Patout's)

Ingredients:
1 pint heavy cream, 1 tablespoon fresh basil, or 2 teaspoons dried, 1 tablespoon fresh thyme, or 2 teaspoons dried, 2 teaspoon salt, 2 teaspoons ground black pepper, 1-1/2 teaspoons ground red pepper, 1 teaspoon ground white pepper, 1 cup chopped green onions, 1 cup chopped parsley, 1/2 pound medium shrimp, peeled and deveined, 1/2 pound crawfish tails, 1/2 pound lump or white crab meat (we use blue crab), 1-1/2 cups grated cheese (Jack, Swiss, and American work well), 2 tablespoons grated Parmesan cheese

Instructions:
Pour the cream into a large heavy skillet or saucepan and place over medium-high heat. The cream will rise before it begins to boil; just stir it to keep it from overflowing. Once it begins to simmer, add the herbs, salt, peppers, green onions, and parsley, and continue to let simmer until it becomes thick, 7-8 minutes. Stir in the shrimp and let cook 3-4 minutes, then add the crawfish. Mix well and let cook 2-3 minutes. Gently fold in the crab meat (you paid a premium price for it, so don't destroy those precious lumps). Let cook 2-3 minutes more, then add the 1-1/2 cups cheese and stir gently until it has melted.

Preheat the broiler. Pour the hot seafood mixture into a large ovenproof dish or individual ramekins. Sprinkle the top with the Parmesan cheese and glaze under the broiler. Serve immediately.

Serves: 6

Additional Notes:
This dish should really be prepared fresh. It doesn't take long to make, and your guests or family will enjoy watching you prepare it. You don't have to use all three kinds of seafood, either. Try it with just one or two of them, increasing the amounts, or substitute other kinds of seafood that are readily available.

Crawfish Etouffee (Alex Patout's)

Ingredients:
1 pound butter, 2 ounces crawfish fat -or as much as you can get your hands on - fresh or frozen, 3 large onions chopped fine, 2 teaspoons salt, 2 bell peppers chopped fine, 2 pounds fresh crawfish tails, 1 cup water, 1 cup finely chopped green onions, 3/4 teaspoon ground red pepper, 1/2 cup finely chopped parsley, 1/2 teaspoon ground black pepper, 1/2 teaspoon ground white pepper

Instructions:
Melt butter in a Dutch oven or other large heavy pot, add the onions and bell peppers, and saute over medium-high heat. Brown well, being sure to scrape the bottom of the pot frequently to loosen any stuck particles. (You want to caramelize the onions to bring out their sweetness.) This process will take about 45 minutes.

Reduce the heat to medium-low and add the salt, peppers, crawfish fat, and water. Stir well and let simmer 30 minutes more. (You can prepare the dish in advance to this point; about 30 minutes before serving, reheat the mixture over medium-high heat.)

Raise the heat to medium, stir in the crawfish, and cook for 10 minutes. then add the green onions and parsley and let cook for another 5 minutes. Place generous servings of hot cooked rice in the middle of large flat plates and spoon the crawfish all around.

Serves: Serves 6.

Additional Notes:
In Cajun Country, crawfish was for a long time considered a poor man's food. the little critters were known as an agricultural pest, and hardly anyone would admit to fixing them at home, let alone be brave enough to put them on a restaurant menu. They finally went public in 1935 when a glorious crawfish etouffee was the first dish served at a levee bar around Henderson called Bernard's. Now crawfish are treated with the respect they deserve - in fact, every other year the little Cajun community of Breaux Bridge swells to over 300,000 people when it holds its International Crawfish Festival the first weekend in May.

Shrimp & Tasso Pasta (From Alex Patout's)

Ingredients:
1 pint heavy cream, 1/2 pound diced tasso or other smoked cured ham (such as Smithfield), 3/4 teaspoon salt, 1/4 teaspoon ground black pepper, 1/4 teaspoon ground red pepper, 1/4 teaspoon ground white pepper, 1/2 cup chopped parsley, 2 teaspoons fresh thyme or 1/2 teaspoon dried, 1 pound spaghetti, 1 pound medium shrimp, 1/2 cup chopped green onions, 2 teaspoons fresh basil, or 1/2 teaspoon dried

Instructions:
Pour the cream into a large heavy skillet and place over medium heat. Stir the cream when it begins to rise to keep it from overflowing; when it comes to a boil, add the tasso, salt, peppers, and herbs and let simmer for 8-10 minutes. You can prepare the sauce ahead to this point. Bring a large pot of salted water to a rolling boil and drop in the pasta. Cook just until al dente.

Meanwhile, return the sauce to a simmer, stir in the shrimp, green onions and parsley and cook just until the shrimp are pink, 3-4 minutes. Drain the pasta and divide among bowls. Spoon the sauce over and serve with Parmesan cheese.

Serves: Serves 4-6 as an entree, 8-10 as an appetizer

CRAWFISH PIE (From Louisiana Foods)

INGREDIENTS
Pie dough enough for 4 individual pies (or 2 large)
1 - 1/2 cups crawfish tails; crawfish fat and water to make 2 cups
3 tablespoons cooking oil
1 medium onion, chopped fine
2 tablespoons butter
1/4 cup chopped celery
Salt and red pepper to taste
1 clove garlic, mashed
Pinch thyme
1/3 cup tomato sauce mixed with 1/3 cup water
Pinch nutmeg
1 tablespoon green onion
4 tablespoons cornstarch
1 tablespoons parsley

INSTRUCTIONS
Cook onion, celery, and garlic in cooking oil, stirring until tender. Dish out half the cooked mixture.
To the mixture, add tomato sauce, water, and crawfish fat, cook over medium heat and when it boils, slowly add cornstarch and water stirring until sauce thickens, season with nutmeg, thyme, red pepper and salt to taste; set aside.
To the remaining cooked onion mixture in a saucepan add crawfish tails, butter, cook 2 to 3 minutes.
Combine sauce, crawfish, green onion and parsley. Cook, then pour into 4 pastry lined pie plates, equally divided. Wet edges of under crust, cover with uppercrust. Press edges together; prick with a fork. Bake in a 450 degree preheated oven 5 minutes; reduce heat to 400 degrees and bake about 15 minutes longer.
COOKING TIP: Be a guest at your own party and prepare these ahead and chill before baking.

Shrimp and Artichoke Linguine (From Tabasco)

* 8 ounces dried linguine pasta
* 2 tablespoons vegetable oil
* 1 medium onion, diced
* 1 large clove garlic, crushed
* 1 pound large shrimp, peeled and deveined
* 1 (9-ounce) package frozen artichoke hearts
* 1 cup white wine or chicken broth
* 2 tablespoons lemon juice
* 2 teaspoons grated lemon peel
* 1 teaspoon TABASCO brand Pepper Sauce
* 1/2 teaspoon salt
* 2 tablespoons chopped fresh parsley

Cook linguine according to package instruction until al dente; drain.

Meanwhile, heat vegetable oil in a 12-inch skillet over medium heat; add onion and garlic and cook until tender, about 5 minutes, stirring occasionally. With a slotted spoon, remove onion to a bowl. Add shrimp to drippings remaining in skillet. Cook over medium-high heat until shrimp turn pink, about 3 minutes.

Stir in frozen artichoke hearts, wine, lemon juice, lemon peel, TABASCO® brand Pepper Sauce, salt and cooked onion and bring to a boil. Reduce heat to low, cover and simmer 5 minutes. Toss with linguine and parsley and serve immediately.

Makes 2 servings.

TROUT MEUNIERE ALMANDINE (From Louisiana Foods)

INGREDIENTS
8 Trout fillets (skinned)
1 Stick of butter (1/4 Pound)
1 Cup flour
1 Juiced Lemon (keep juice)
2 Teaspoons of salt or to taste.
¼ Cup of chopped parsley (Flat leaf preferably)
3 Teaspoons of red pepper or to taste.
½ Cup roasted sliced almonds (Roast at 375 degrees 7 minutes)

INSTRUCTIONS
Sprinkle trout fillets with seasoning then dredge in flour. Melt butter in shallow skillet; add fish and cook slowly until golden brown on both sides. Remove fish from skillet and set in oven to keep warm. Add lemon juice and parsley to butter and drippings in the skillet. Mix well then poor over cooked fish fillets. Sprinkle sliced almond over the fillets.
4 Servings

CAJUN-STYLE SEAFOOD BAKED EGGPLANT (From Feelings Cafe)

INGREDIENTS
1/2 cup butter
1/4 pound hot link sausage, diced
1/4 pound chicken gizzards, diced
3 medium eggplants, peeled and diced
3 green bell peppers, seeded and chopped
3 medium onions, chopped
2 garlic cloves, minced
1 bunch green onions, chopped
1/2 cup celery, chopped
1/2 pound fresh small shrimp, peeled and deveined
1 cup cooked rice
1/4 cup fresh parsley, chopped
1 teaspoon Italian seasoning
Salt to taste
1/2 pound lump crabmeat
1/3 to 1/2 cup Italian bread crumbs
2 to 3 tablespoons butter
Lemon slices and chopped fresh parsley for garnish

INSTRUCTIONS
Melt 1/2 cup butter in Dutch oven or large saucepan over medium-high heat. Add sausage and gizzards and saute until browned, about 5 minutes. Stir in eggplant, bell pepper, onion, garlic, green onion and celery. Continue to cook about 15 minutes, stir-ring occasionally. Add shrimp, rice, parsley, Italian seasoning and salt. Cook, stirring occasionally, until shrimp is pink and translucent, about 15 minutes. Remove from heat. Preheat oven to 350 degrees. Add crabmeat to eggplant mixture with enough bread crumbs to absorb remaining butter. Spoon into individual ramekins. Sprinkle with remaining bread crumbs and dot with butter. Bake until tops are browned. Garnish with lemon and parsley. Serve immediately.

Serves 8 to 10.

REDFISH PARMESAN (From Louisiana Foods)

INGREDIENTS
6 Redfish Fillets (8 - 10 ounces)
2 cups Half & Half Cream
2 eggs
1 cup of flour
2 tsp. White Pepper
3/4 cup Cracker Meal
2/3 cup Parmesan Cheese
1/2 teaspoon Paprika
2 tablespoons Oregano
1 tablespoon Basil
2 tablespoons Parsley
1/2 teaspoon Cayenne Pepper
1 cup Olive Oil
1/4 pound Butter (unsalted)
2 Lemons, cut in wedges, for garnish

INSTRUCTIONS
Combine all ingredients except the flour, half & half cream, eggs, oil and butter. Dust the fillets in the flour, then dip in cream and egg mixture. Coat with all of the other dry ingredients combined. Saute in olive oil and butter on medium high heat until fillets are golden and fish starts to flake. Garnish with lemon and parsley.

Soft-Shell Crab (From Stella! Restaurant)

Makes 4 servings

4 Louisiana soft-shell crabs, dressed
1 egg
1 cup milk
peanut oil, for frying
1 cup all-purpose flour, in all
2 cups corn flour
salt, to taste
cayenne pepper, to taste

Preheat oven to 150°F. Heat peanut oil to 325°F. Whisk together egg and milk. Mix corn flour with 2/3 cup all-purpose flour and season with salt and cayenne pepper. Season crab and dust with 1/3 cup flour, then egg-wash, then corn flour mixture. Fry crab until golden brown, about 5 to 7 minutes. Keep warm in a 150°F oven.

Note: The eyes and gills in the soft shell crabs must be removed before cooking.

Crab Meat Broussard (From Broussard's Restaurant)

Ingredients:
1 tbsp. butter
6 jumbo shrimp, peeled, tail left on, deveined; butterfly
1 oz. (2 tbsp.) olive oil
1 small yellow onion, diced
2 fresh artichoke hearts, chopped
1 large clove garlic, minced
1/4 cup flour
1/4 cup white wine
2 cups chicken stock
1 cup heavy cream
3 oz. brie cheese
1/2 cup bread crumbs
3 tbsp. olive oil
1 tbsp. whole fresh thyme leaves
3/4 lb. jumbo lump crab meat

Directions:

Preheat the oven to 400 degrees.
In a large skillet, melt the butter and sauté the shrimp until they are just cooked. Set aside to cool.
In a heavy saucepan, heat the olive oil and sauté the yellow onion, artichoke hearts, and garlic over medium heat until the onion becomes limp.
Sprinkle in the flour and mix well while cooking for a minute more.
Deglaze the pan with the white wine, then add stock.
Bring to a boil, reduce heat, and simmer for three minutes.
Add the heavy cream and simmer for another five minutes.
Take the brie and scrape off and discard the white skin; cut cheese into small pieces.
Add brie to the ream sauce and stir until all of the cheese is melted and mixed well.
Remove from heat and allow to cool.
In a small bowl, combine the bread crumbs, olive oil, and thyme.
Set aside.
After the cheese mixture is cool, gently fold in the crab meat, being careful not break up the lumps.
To assemble, place one shrimp in the center of an oven proof serving dish so that it stands.
Spoon the crab meat mixture around the shrimp and sprinkle with the bread crumb mixture.
Repeat with the remaining shrimp.
Arrange the dishes on a large baking pan and bake in the preheated oven for fifteen minutes, or until the crab mixture is hot and bubbly. Serve immediately. Serves 6.

Lobster with Truffle Butter (From Bacco's Restaurant)

Ingredients:
4 each, 1 1/2 pound, Fresh Lobsters
16 ounces, Truffle Butter Sauce (see below)
20 each, Asparagus Spears, blanched
1 sprig, Italian flay leaf parsley
Shaved Italian White truffles, optional
1 ounce, Unsalted Butter
Salt and Pepper

Directions:
In a pot heavily salted, boiling water, drop the live lobsters in and cook for about 6 minutes (4 minutes per pound of lobster).
Pull lobster from water and pull claws off and crack carefully trying to keep them whole and set aside.
With a large knife, split the lobster in half from head to tail.
Heat the asparagus spears in a sauté pan with butter, salt and pepper to taste.
Place the lobster on an entree plate with the asparagus and claws. Drizzle with truffle butter sauce.
Garnish with a sprig of Italian parsley.
To truly make this a special dish, add fresh Italian white shaved truffles.

Truffle Butter Sauce:
1/2 ounce, Olive Oil
4 each, Shallots, minced
1/4 cup, Rice Vinegar
1/4 cup, Heavy Cream
1 pound, Unsalted Butter, cut into Tablespoons, room temp
1/2 ounce, White Truffle Oil
1/2 ounce, Black Truffle slices packed in oil
Salt and Pepper to taste

Directions:
In a heavy bottom sauce pot add olive oil and place over med-high heat.
Add minced shallots and sauté until translucent.
Add rice vinegar and white wine and reduce until syrupy consistency.
Add heavy cream and reduce until thick and syrupy.
Turn heat down to medium and begin to whisk in butter until fully incorporated.
Finish sauce by adding truffle oil, sliced truffles and salt and pepper.
Set the sauce aside until ready to use. Sauce must be kept in a warm place- not too hot or too cold or sauce will break.
Serves Four

Oysters Louisiana (From Acme Oyster House Restaurant)

Ingredients:
4 oz. butter - melted
1.5 pints oysters - drained
4 green onions - chopped finely
3 cloves garlic - minced
½ lb. fresh lump crabmeat
½ cup bread crumbs
Salt and pepper to taste

Directions:
Melt butter in a skillet. Add oysters and cook until dry. Add onions and garlic and cook slowly for at least 10 minutes. Fold in crabmeat and crumbs. Simmer 5 minutes more. Add salt and pepper to taste.

Shrimp Ravioli Bay Eloi in Shrimp Herb Essence (From Rib Room Restaurant)

Ingredients:
6 Pieces Shrimp Ravioli
4 oz Shrimp Stock
4 oz Whole Softened Butter
½ tsp Shallots Chopped
½ tsp Garlic Chopped
2 oz White Wine
3 oz Diced Tomatoes
½ tsp Parsley Chopped
½ tsp Tarragon Chopped
½ tsp Chives Chopped
3 Pieces 10-15 Count Shrimp Grilled
4 oz French Spinach Sautéed in Butter
Method:
Sweat shallots and garlic in olive oil
Add white wine and reduce by half
Add shrimp stock and reduce by half
Incorporate the butter by whipping in with a wire whip
Finish with diced tomatoes and herbs
Blanch ravioli in boiling water for 3 minutes
Drain and set aside
For Plate:
In large bowl, add sautéed spinach
Arrange ravioli on top of spinach
Spoon sauce around ravioli. Garnish with grilled shrimp and herb sprigs

Baked oysters RioMar (From RioMar Restaurant)

Makes 6 servings

2 teaspoons olive oil

4 links Spanish chorizo, ground

½ medium onion, chopped

3 tablespoons chopped garlic

2 cups cooked spinach

½ cup bread crumbs

½ cup grated Manchego cheese

Salt and pepper

24 shucked oysters

Butter

Heat olive oil and brown chorizo with onion and garlic. Cool mixture. Chop cooked spinach and combine it with most of the cheese and bread crumbs. (Save a little of the bread crumbs for topping.) Add cooled chorizo mix and season to taste with salt and pepper.

Fill individual ramekins (or a baking pan coated with nonstick spray) with half the chorizo mix and put oysters on top. Cover with remaining mixture and sprinkle with rest of bread crumbs. Top each ramekin with small dabs of butter so the bread crumbs will brown.

Bake in 400-degree oven until brown.

Grilled redfish and crabmeat with lemon-butter sauce (From Ralph Brennan's New Orleans Classic Seafood)

¼ cup dry white wine plus a few tablespoons
6 (6 to 8 ounce) skinless redfish fillets, neatly trimmed
2 tablespoons Creole seasoning
4 tablespoons unsalted butter
1 pound jumbo lump crabmeat, picked over
1 teaspoon kosher salt
‰ teaspoon freshly ground black pepper

Clean the grill well and preheat to hot. Add wet or dry hickory or other wood chips. Brush rack with a thick wad of paper towels saturated in salad oil, holding it with long-handled tongs.
While the grill is preheating, prepare lemon-butter sauce (below) and keep warm.
Brush both sides of fillets with salad oil and season evenly with ½ teaspoon Creole seasoning on each side of each fillet.
When grill is hot place fillets on it and cook about 2½ to 4 minutes per side, turning once. Watch closely so the fish does not overcook. When you think fish is approaching doneness you prefer, insert the tip of a knife into the thicket part of the fillet, then lay the tip of the blade flat against the inside of your wrist. If the tip feels hot, the fish should be done.
(If cooking in batches, transfer to a heat-proof platter and drizzle with white wine to keep them moist; keep in a warm spot.)
While the fillets are grilling, saute crabmeat. In a heavy 12-inch saute pan, melt butter over medium-high heat until hot, about 3 minutes. Add ¼ cup wine and heat 30 seconds. Add crabmeat; season with 1 teaspoon kosher salt and ‰ teaspoon pepper. Cook until crabmeat is just warmed through, about 2 minutes, lightly tossing so lumps of crabmeat stay intact. Serve immediately.
Arrange a fish fillet on a heated dinner plate; top with a portion of crabmeat and spoon 3 tablespoons sauce over it.

Lemon-butter sauce
1½ cups good-quality dry white wine
½ cup fresh lemon juice
½ teaspoon minced lemon zest
1 teaspoon cider vinegar
1 teaspoon minced shallots
1 teaspoon minced garlic
1 teaspoon, packed, minced fresh thyme leaves
2 tablespoons heavy cream
1 pound (3.5 sticks) cold unsalted butter, cut into about 20 pats
1 teaspoon kosher salt, or to taste
¼ teaspoon freshly ground black pepper, or to taste   >

In a heavy 3-quart saucepan, combine wine, lemon juice and zest, vinegar, shallots, garlic and thyme. Cook over medium-high heat until the liquid in the mixture reduces to 1 to 2 tablespoons, about 5 minutes. Add cream and cook until liquid is reduced to 1 to 2 tablespoons, about 4 minutes.

(The sauce may be prepared to this point up to 45 minutes ahead and left at room temperature. Reheat briefly over medium heat, whisking constantly, before proceeding.) Reduce heat to medium-low and add 2 pats of butter at a time, whisking constantly, until all butter is incorporated. Each addition should be almost melted before adding more, so this will take about 10 to 15 minutes total. Remove from heat

Whisk in salt and pepper. If serving immediately, strain through a fine-mesh strainer into a small saucepan. If not, strain into the top of a double boiler and serve as soon as possible (definitely within one hour), keeping the sauce warm, uncovered, over hot (not simmering) water.   6 servings.

Soft-shell crab with meuniere sauce and a nutty option (From Galatoire's)

Sauteed soft-shell crabs
Makes 1 serving

2 large soft-shell crabs
Flour
Salt and pepper
1 stick butter, clarified
2 sticks salted butter
Juice of 1 lemon
1 tablespoon red wine vinegar
Finely chopped parsley
Thinly sliced lemons
2 to 3 tablespoons toasted sliced almonds (optional)
About ½ cup jumbo lump crab (optional)

Prepare soft-shell crabs: Remove bottom flap, lungs, and eyes.

Spread flour in a flat pan and season with salt and pepper. Dust crabs in the flour. Let them sit in the flour while you heat a large saute pan.

Add about half the clarified butter to the heated pan. When butter is hot, add crabs. Saute until nicely browned on both sides, turning once. When browned, remove to a heated plate and keep warm.

Make meuniere sauce: To the same saute pan, over high heat, add salted butter. Cook until it is brown (not black) and smells nutty. Remove from heat and add the lemon juice and red wine. Combine well. Taste and correct the seasoning with salt and pepper. Drizzle the sauce over the crabs on the plate. Garnish with parsley and lemon wheels.

Optional: Make it soft-shell meuniere amandine. Add a little more clarified butter to a different, clean skillet, over very low heat. Add jumbo lump crabmeat and toss briefly. Season with salt and pepper.

Sprinkle almonds over soft-shells and top with the jumbo lump crabmeat. Serve immediately.

Maine Lobster a la Pittari (From Pittari's)

Makes 4 servings

2 tablespoons olive oil

1/2 cup finely chopped green onions

1/2 cup finely chopped celery

2 cloves garlic, finely chopped

1/2 cup chopped cooked shrimp

1/2 cup fresh lump crabmeat (back fin)

1/4 cup finely chopped parsley

2 cups bread crumbs

Salt and pepper

2 2-1/2 pound lobsters, split in half lengthwise

Paprika

Melted butter

Pour olive oil into skillet and heat. Add green onions, celery and garlic. Marinate until soft, not brown. Add chopped shrimp, let simmer until cooked (sic), stirring gently to keep from sticking. Add lump carbmeat and stir gently. Add salt and pepper to taste. Let simmer about 20 minutes. Stir in parsley and bread crumbs.

Parboil lobsters 2 minutes to the pound. Clean cavity in the head, fill with dressing, and sprinkle lightly with paprika. Brush the entire lobster with melted butter. Place in broiler for about 20 minutes.

Le Petit's blue crab baked in brie cream (From Le Petit's Grocerie)

Blue crab baked in brie cream
Makes 2 servings

½ cup heavy cream
2 ounces jumbo lump Louisiana blue crab
2 ounces brie cheese
Snipped chives
Salt and pepper to taste
¼ cup grated reggiano parmesan
1/8 cup of panko bread crumbs
Warm bread for serving
Preheat broiler to high.

In a small sauce pan, reduce cream by half over medium-high heat. Add crab and simmer until warmed through. Gently fold in brie and some of the chives. Taste for salt and pepper; adjust seasoning.
Transfer mixture to a greased 8-ounce casserole dish and top with half the parmesan, the panko, then the rest of the parmesan.
Place in broiler for 25 to 30 seconds, until golden brown.
Garnish with more chives, and serve with warm bread.

New Orleans sauteed shrimp with farfalle pasta, tomato and basil (From Emeril's)

Emeril's New Orleans sauteed shrimp with farfalle pasta, tomato and basil
Makes 4 to 6 servings
2 tablespoons olive oil
2 pounds fresh Gulf shrimp, peeled and deveined
Emeril's Original Essence seasoning
Kosher salt and freshly ground black pepper, to taste
1 tablespoon minced shallots
1 ½ teaspoons minced garlic
1 cup peeled, seeded, diced fresh tomatoes
1 pound farfalle pasta, cooked al dente, drained
4 ounces unsalted butter
¼ cup chiffonade or finely chopped, fresh basil
Heat a large saute pan over medium high heat and add the olive oil.
Season the shrimp on both sides with Essence, salt, and pepper.
When the oil is hot, add the shrimp and cook until golden on one side, 1 to 2 minutes.
Turn the shrimp over, add the shallots and garlic and continue to cook till fragrant, about 1 minute longer. Do not allow shallots and garlic to brown.
Add tomato and cook until they have released some of their liquid, about 2 minutes.
Reduce the heat to low and add the pasta, stirring constantly until just heated through.
Add the butter little by little, stirring constantly until completely incorporated. Do not allow the sauce to boil.
Remove from the heat, add the basil, and stir to combine. Season to taste with salt and pepper and serve immediately.

Trout meuniere (From Brigtsen's)

Trout meuniere with shrimp and roasted pecans

Makes 2 servings

2 eggs
2 cups milk
2 cups all-purpose flour
5 to 6 teaspoons Chef Paul Prudhomme's Seafood Magic seasoning
2 five-ounce speckled trout filets
½ cup vegetable or peanut oil
1 tablespoon plus 4 tablespoons unsalted butter, softened
6 medium-sized peeled fresh shrimp
½ cup roasted pecan pieces
2 tablespoons thinly sliced green onions
¼ teaspoon minced fresh garlic
½ teaspoon Lea & Perrins Worcestershire sauce
6 tablespoons shrimp stock
½ teaspoon lemon juice

In a mixing bowl, whisk eggs until frothy. Whisk in milk until fully blended. Transfer the mixture to a shallow pan and set aside.

In a separate shallow pan, place flour and 4 teaspoons of the seafood seasoning. Blend well and set aside.

Heat oil in a 12-inch skillet over medium-high heat. Season both sides of the fish filets, lightly and evenly, with the seafood seasoning. (Use about ¾ teaspoon seasoning per filet.)

When the oil is hot, dredge the fish filets in the seasoned flour, then in the egg/milk wash, then back in the flour. Immediately place each battered fish filet into the hot oil. Cook the fish, turning once, until both sides are brown and crispy, 2 to 3 minutes per side.

Transfer cooked fish to a sheet pan lined with paper towels to drain. Keep warm while you make the sauce.

Discard the oil, reserving any browned bits of flour in the bottom of the pan. Return the skillet to the stove over high heat.

Add 1 tablespoon of the softened butter and cook, shaking the skillet constantly until the butter turns dark brown, 10 to 20 seconds. Add the shrimp and cook just until the shrimp turn pink on the outside. >

Add the pecans, green onions, garlic and ¼ teaspoon of seafood seasoning. Cook, shaking the skillet constantly, for 10 seconds. Add the Lea & Perrins, stock and lemon juice. Bring the mixture to a boil. Add the remaining 4 tablespoons of butter. Reduce heat to low and cook, shaking the skillet vigorously back and forth, just until the butter melts into the sauce and becomes emulsified. Remove from heat.

To serve, place 1 trout filet on each serving plate and top each filet with 3 shrimp and ¼ cup of sauce. Serve immediately.

Shrimp, scallop and salmon "farci" with risotto (From The Bistro at the Maison de Ville)

FARCI
1 to 2 tablespoons extra-virgin olive oil
8 large shrimp
4 to 6 large scallops
6 4-ounce portions salmon
1 teaspoon minced garlic
½ teaspoon soy sauce
Squeeze of lemon juice
1 red and 1 green bell pepper, roasted, peeled, chopped
Salt and pepper to taste
RISOTTO
½ cup extra virgin olive oil
1 pound arborio rice
1 large onion, chopped
1 cup white wine
1 quart chicken stock
1 pound Italian sausage, sliced
1 cup pistachios
1 teaspoon garlic, minced
2 cups fresh or frozen green peas
1 tablespoon Worcestershire sauce
SAUCE
1 to 2 tablespoons extra-virgin olive oil
1 small fennel bulb, finely diced
2 teaspoons minced garlic
½ cup white wine
1 generous pinch saffron threads
1 quart chicken stock
½ ear corn, roasted, kernels cut off
2 large Roma or 1 large Creole tomato, diced
2 tablespoons chopped parsley
½ pound (2 sticks) unsalted butter

FARCI: Preheat oven to 475 degrees. Heat 1 to 2 tablespoons extra-virgin olive oil and saute shrimp and scallops until halfway cooked. Add garlic, soy, lemon and some half roasted peppers. Mix well.
Slice salmon along edge to form pocket. Stuff with seafood mixture. Place salmon pieces cut-side down on greased baking pan. Sprinkle with salt and pepper. Roast at 475 degrees for 8 minutes, until salmon is medium rare.
RISOTTO: Heat olive oil in a large skillet and saute onion over high heat in for 2 to 3 minutes. Add dry rice. Toss in oil, then deglaze pan with white wine. Continue cooking >

over high heat, adding stock about a cup at a time and Worcestershire sauce, stirring constantly, until rice is al dente. Remove from heat.

In another pan, saute sausage until cooked through. Add pistachios, garlic and peas. Adjust seasoning. Fold into cooked risotto.

SAUCE: Heat 1 to 2 tablespoons oil and saute fennel and minced garlic until tender. Add wine, saffron, and stock. Cook for 5 minutes. Add corn. Cook until liquid is reduced by one-third. Add tomatoes and parsley and cook 3 more minutes. Add butter just prior to serving.

TO PLATE: Place portion of risotto on bottom of plate or shallow bowl. Stack seafood-stuffed salmon (pocket side down) atop risotto, then ladle butter broth around dish and over salmon. 6 servings.

Soft Shell Crab Doré (From Broussard's)

Ingredients:

Sauce Doré:
1 lb. cleaned shrimp
1 cup sliced mushrooms
1/4 cup chopped shallots
1/2 white wine
1/2 cup heavy cream
1/4 cup lemon juice
1/4 cup green onions
1/2 tsp. chopped garlic
1/4 cup butter, salt, and pepper

Method:
Sprinkle salt, pepper, and lemon juice on cleaned crabs. Sauté in butter until crabs turn red. Set aside on a dish and keep warm.

Sauté shrimp in wine for 2-3 minutes, add shallots, green onions, mushrooms, lemon juice, and garlic. Slowly cook for 3 minutes, add heavy cream and butter. Cook until it becomes a sauce, add salt and pepper to taste. On 6 warm plates put sauce in center of plate topping with warm crabs. Garnish with chopped parsley, lemon slices, and fresh dill sprig.

Serves 6

Crab Meat Broussard (From Broussard's)

Ingredients:

- 1 tbsp. butter
- 6 jumbo shrimp, peeled, tail left on, de-veined; butterfly
- 1 oz. (2 tbsp.) olive oil
- 1 small yellow onion, diced
- 2 fresh artichoke hearts, chopped
- 1 large clove garlic, minced
- 1/4 cup flour
- 1/4 cup white wine
- 2 cups chicken stock
- 1 cup heavy cream
- 3 oz. brie cheese
- 1/2 cup bread crumbs
- 3 tbsp. olive oil
- 1 tbsp. whole fresh thyme leaves
- 3/4 lb. jumbo lump crab meat

Method:
Preheat the oven to 400 degrees. In a large skillet, melt the butter and sauté the shrimp until they are just cooked. Set aside to cool

In a heavy saucepan, heat the olive oil and sauté the yellow onion, artichoke hearts, and garlic over medium heat until the onion becomes limp. Sprinkle in the flour and mix well while cooking for a minute more. Deglaze the pan with the white wine, then add stock. Bring to a boil, reduce heat, and simmer for three minutes. Add the heavy cream and simmer for another five minutes.

Take the brie and scrape off and discard the white skin; cut cheese into small pieces. Add brie to the ream sauce and stir until all of the cheese is melted and mixed well. Remove from heat and allow to cool.

In a small bowl, combine the bread crumbs, olive oil, and thyme. Set aside. After the cheese mixture is cool, gently fold in the crab meat, being careful not break up the lumps.

To assemble, place one shrimp in the center of an oven proof serving dish so that it stands. Spoon the crab meat mixture around the shrimp and sprinkle with the bread crumb mixture. Repeat with the remaining shrimp.

Arrange the dishes on a large baking pan and bake in the preheated oven for fifteen minutes, or until the crab mixture is hot and bubbly. Serve immediately.
Serves 6

Filet of Trout Marcus (From Broussard's)

Ingredients:

- 6 6-oz. filets
- Salt
- White pepper
- Lemon juice
- All-purpose flour
- 5 whole eggs, beaten
- 3/4 cup clarified margarine
- Marcus Garnish
- 2 tbsp. chopped parsley

Method:
Season the trout filets with the salt, white pepper, and lemon juice. Dredge them in the flour; shake off any excess. Dip the floured filets in the beaten eggs, then sauté them in hot clarified margarine until the edges begin to brown. Turn the fish over and cook gently until it flakes easily, about 5 minutes.

Serve the trout with the Marcus Garnish spooned over them, garnished with chopped parsley.

Filet of Trout Marcus Garnish

Ingredients:
- 6 fresh, trimmed and cooked artichoke bottoms; or 1 14-oz. can artichoke bottoms
- 2 tbsp. sliced green onions
- 1/2 tsp. chopped garlic
- 1/2 tsp. chopped dry shallots
- 3 tbsp. "nonpareil" capers, or other select small capers, rinsed
- 1/2 cup white wine
- 1/2 cup fresh lemon juice
- 1 cup fresh butter
- Salt ot taste
- White pepper to taste

Method:
In a saucepan, combine the artichoke bottoms with the green onions, garlic, shallots, capers, white wine, and lemon juice. Bring to a boil. Divide the butter into three pieces and add all at once. Swirl and agitate in the pan until the butter is fully emulsified. Season to taste with the salt and white pepper.
Do not let the sauce overheat at this point, not even to a simmer. If the sauce simmers, the butter will separate and the sauce will thin out. The sauce needs to remain creamy from the butter. Serves 6

Salmon De La Salle (From Broussard's)

Ingredients:

* 3 lemon slices
* 4 1-oz. sliced salmon
* 4 plum tomatoes (skin off)
* 1/2 green pepper
* 1/2 cucumber
* 1/4 white onion
* 3 cloves garlic
* 3 oz. tomato juice
* Pinch chopped parsley
* 1 1/2 oz. olive oil
* Juice of one lemon
* Pinch salt
* Pinch black pepper
* Tabasco
* Pinch cumin

Method:
In a blender, combine whole tomatoes, green pepper, cucumber, garlic, onion, tomato juice, parsley, black pepper, olive oil, lemon juice, and cumin.

Blend fast so mixture remains coarse, add Tabasco to taste, pour into serving plate.

In a hot skillet, sear your thin slices of salmon, remove from skillet and place on top of sauce. Garnish with lemon slices and parsley sprigs.

Serves 2

Lobster Thermidor Recipe (From NolaCuisine.com- Danno's Recipe)

For the Lobsters:
2 1-1/4 lb Lobsters
Whole lemons
4 Bay Leaves
4 Tbsp Creole Seasoning
2 Tbsp Black peppercorns
1 Bunch Thyme, tied together
1/4 Cup Kosher Salt
Water, enough to cover 2 lobsters

Combine all of the ingredients except the Lobsters, bring to a rolling boil. Cook for 15 mintes. While still boiling drop the lobsters into the pot. Cook for 5-6 minutes, remove immediately to an ice water bath to stop the cooking process. I like to under cook the lobsters so they will finish cooking in the sauce.
When the lobsters are cold, remove both claws from the body. Cut the body in half lengthwise. Extract all of the tail meat, and all of the meat from the claws and knuckles. Cut the meat into nice sized chunks. Totally clean out the shells and place face down on a baking sheet. Place in a 300 degree oven to dry them out, when dry, remove and set aside on a clean baking sheet.

For the Sauce:
4 Tbsp Unsalted Butter
4 Tbsp Shallots, finely minced
1 Tbsp Garlic, finely minced
4 Tbsp Flour
1/4 Cup Sherry
1/2 Cup Whole milk
3/4 Cup Heavy Cream
2 tsp Dijon Mustard
pinch of freshly grated nutmeg
pinch of Cayenne
1/4 Cup shredded Gruyere cheese
1/4 Cup shredded Parmesan
1 Tbsp fresh Tarragon, minced
2 Tbsp Italian Parsley, minced
Kosher salt and white pepper to taste

Melt the butter in a small heavy bottomed saucepan. Sweat the shallots and garlic until translucent. Whisk in the flour and cook to make a blond roux, whisk in the Sherry. Cook for one minute, stirring constantly. Slowly whisk in the milk, then move on to the cream. Add the dijon, cayenne and nutmeg. Bring to a boil, then reduce to a simmer, stirring constantly, to prevent scorching. Cook just until the raw flour taste is gone, remove >

from the heat. While still hot whisk in 3/4 of each cheese, stir until incorporated. Stir in the Tarragon and parsley. Season to taste with Kosher salt & white pepper.

Preheat the oven to 400 degrees F.

Mix the reserved lobster meat with some of the sauce (you may not need all of the sauce). The result should be very plentiful with lobster meat. Fill the reserved shells with the prepared sauce. Top with the remaining Gruyere and Parmesan. If you have a little sauce sauce with lobster leftover, bake it off in a small casserole or ramekin.

Bake until the cheese and sauce are nicely golden brown, serve on top of something green, I used Chicory.

I like to serve this with toast points. Serves 2.

Redfish Courtbouillon Recipe (From NolaCuisine.com - Danno's Recipe)

2 Whole Redfish, Red Snapper, or other firm fleshed fish (scaled, gutted and trimmed of all fins)
1 Cup Flour, liberally seasoned with salt, pepper and cayenne
2 Tbsp Unsalted butter
1/4 Cup dry white wine
1 Recipe Creole Sauce, made with fish stock, and made extra thick
1 Lemon, thinly sliced
2 bunches fresh Thyme, 1/2 of which tied tightly with butcher's twine
1 Bay Leaf
1 Recipe Creole Boiled Rice as an accompaniment

Season the fish all over including in the cavity with kosher salt, black pepper and a little cayenne. Place some of the sliced lemon and 1/2 of the Thyme into the cavity of each fish.
Dredge the fish in the seasoned flour and warm the unsalted butter in a large cast iron skillet.
When the butter just starts to brown place the fish in the pan, cook until golden brown on both sides.
Remove the fish to a plate and deglaze the pan with the white wine. When the wine reduces slightly, add the fish back to the pan and ladle enough Creole Sauce to come up the sides of the fish by half, plus ladle a little on top of the fish.
Add the Thyme and bay leaf to the pan and place some of the lemon slices on top of the fish. Cover the pan with a lid or aluminum foil and place into a 350 degree over for 30 minutes.

When plating, carefully remove the fish and filet gently being careful to get rid of all of the bones. An alternate method would be to filet the fish raw and use the head and bones to make your fish stock.

Serve with Creole Boiled Rice and garnish with chopped parsley, lemon slices, and a genourous helping of the Creole Sauce from the pan.

Serves 2-4 depending on the size of your fish.

Seafood Sauce Piquante (From Chef John Folse)

Prep Time: 1½ Hours
Yields: 6-8 Servings

Comment:
The foundation of sauce piquante definitely came from the early Spanish. Since then, the popular dish has been altered by the Cajuns of bayou country and is often made with seafood.

Ingredients:

* 1 pound (21-25 count) shrimp, peeled and deveined1 pound jumbo
* lump crabmeat
* 1 pint select oysters in liquid
* 1 pound redfish, cubed
* ½ cup oil
* ½ cup flour
* 1 cup diced onions
* 1 cup diced celery
* 1 cup diced bell peppers
* 2 tbsps minced garlic
* 1 (8-ounce) can tomato sauce
* 1 cup diced tomatoes
* 1 tbsp minced jalapeños
* 2 whole bay leaves
* ½ tsp thyme
* ½ tsp basil
* 1 ½ quarts fish stock
* 1 cup sliced green onions
* 1 cup chopped parsley
* salt and cracked black pepper to taste

Method:
In a 1-gallong heavy-bottomed saucepot, heat oil over medium-high heat. Whisk in flour, stirring constantly until dark brown roux is achieved. Add onions, celery, bell pepper and garlic. Sauté 3-5 minutes or until vegetables are wilted. Stir in diced tomatoes and jalapeños. Blend well then add bay leaves, thyme and basil. Slowly add fish stock, one ladle at a time, stirring constantly until all is incorporated. Bring to a low boil, reduce to simmer and cook 30 minutes. Add additional fish stock if necessary to retain volume. Add fish, shrimp, oysters and oyster liquid and continue to cook 5-10 additional minutes. Add green onions and parsley. Season to taste using salt and pepper. When shrimp are pink and curled, carefully fold in lump crabmeat. Adjust seasonings if necessary. Serve over hot white rice or pasta.

Valentine's Creole Fish en Papillote (From Chef John Folse)

Prep Time: 45 Minutes
Yields: 2 Servings

Comment:
This classic dish is perfect for a romantic Valentine's Day dinner and can be prepared by even the most novice cook. The cooking method gives the fish a wonderful flavor and provides a very dramatic presentation. We've given the dish a Louisiana twist by cooking the fish in a rich Creole sauce with shrimp and crawfish.

Ingredients:

- 2 (8-ounce) tilapia fillets (other fish may be used, such as trout, redfish, drum, etc.)
- ½ cup diced onions
- ¼ cup diced celery
- ¼ cup diced bell peppers
- 1 tbsp minced garlic
- 1-2 tbsp olive oil
- ½ pound (26-30 count) shrimp
- 4 ounces Louisiana crawfish tails
- 1 medium can diced tomatoes, drained
- 1 cup tomato sauce
- 1 tsp sugar
- 1 tsp each chopped basil, thyme or oregano (optional)
- salt and black pepper to taste

Method:
Preheat oven to 400°F. In a small saucepan, sauté onions, celery, bell peppers, and garlic in olive oil over medium heat for about 5 minutes. Add shrimp and crawfish and continue to cook for about 5 minutes or until shrimp turn opaque. Add tomatoes, tomato sauce and sugar. Stir in herbs if desired. You may use any combination of basil, thyme and oregano. Simmer for about 5 minutes. Season to taste with salt and pepper and set aside. Cut 2 pieces of parchment or waxed paper into 12-inch squares. Fold in half and cut into a semi-circle so that when unfolded it is shaped like a heart. Brush entire paper with olive or vegetable oil. Season fish with salt and black pepper and place on one half of paper. Top each piece of fish with half the sauce, making sure each piece gets an equal amount of seafood. Fold paper over and starting at one end, make small folds overlapping each other, forming a completely sealed pouch. Brush outside of paper with oil and bake about 20 minutes or until paper is golden brown. Cut bag open right before serving, taking care not to burn anyone with steam.

Crawfish Au Gratin (From Chef John Folse)

PREP TIME: 45 Minutes
SERVES: 6

COMMENT:
Au gratins of many types are found on menus throughout Louisiana. The dish is most commonly made with jumbo lump crabmeat. Although, normally served casserole-style, I have also seen it served as the perfect topping over a sauteed filet of fish. Additionally, au gratins make excellent hors d'oeuvres and can be served with garlic croutons or crackers.

INGREDIENTS:

- 1 pound crawfish tails
- 1/4 pound butter
- 1/4 cup onions, diced
- 1/4 cup celery, diced
- 1/4 cup red bell pepper, chopped
- 1/4 cup yellow bell pepper, chopped
- 1 tbsp garlic, diced
- 2 tbsps flour
- 2 cups heavy whipping cream
- 1 ounce dry white wine
- 1 tbsp lemon juice
- dash of hot sauce
- 3/4 cup grated cheddar cheese
- salt and cracked black pepper to taste
- 1/4 cup green onions, sliced
- 1/4 cup parsley, chopped

METHOD:
Preheat oven to 375 degrees F. In a heavy-bottomed 2-quart sauce pan, melt butter over medium-high heat. Add onions, celery, red and yellow bell peppers and garlic. Sauté 3 to 5 minutes or until vegetables are wilted. Be careful not to brown vegetables. Add 1/2 pound crawfish tails and saute 3 additional minutes. Sprinkle in flour, blending well into the mixture. Using a wire whip, whisk cream into sauce pan stirring constantly until thick cream sauce is achieved. Reduce heat to simmer, add white wine, lemon juice and hot sauce. Sprinkle in half of the cheddar cheese stirring the mixture constantly. Season to taste using salt and pepper. Add green onions and parsley for color. If mixture becomes too thick, add a small amount of hot water or whipping cream. Place equal parts of remaining crawfish tails in the bottom of six au gratin dishes, top with sauce and sprinkle with remaining cheddar cheese. Bake for 15 minutes or until cheese is bubbly.

Crawfish Omelette (From Chef John Folse)

PREP TIME: 30 Minutes
SERVES: 6

COMMENT:
Nothing is more appropriate for a breakfast or brunch buffet than a full-flavored omelette. The Cajuns have their own version of this dish and it normally includes fresh seasonal seafood. When combined with colored peppers and a touch of garlic, crawfish makes the best of the Cajun omelettes, in my opinion.

INGREDIENTS:

* 1 lb cooked crawfish tails
* ¼ cup butter
* ¼ cup minced red bell pepper
* 1 tbsp chopped garlic
* ½ cup sliced mushrooms
* ¼ cup sliced green onions
* 1 tbsp chopped parsley
* 8 eggs
* ½ cup milk
* salt and cracked black pepper to taste
* ½ tsp Worcestershire sauce

METHOD:
In a heavy-bottomed sauté pan, heat butter over medium high heat. Add bell pepper, garlic, mushrooms and green onions. Sauté three to five minutes or until vegetables are wilted. Add crawfish, green onions and parsley. Continue to sauté an additional five minutes. In a small mixing bowl, place eggs and milk. Using a wire whisk, beat until well blended. Season to taste using salt, pepper and Worcestershire. Pour egg / milk mixture over crawfish and stir gently. When eggs are set, turn omelette onto a platter. Garnish with fresh parsley.

Stuffed Eggplant with Shrimp (From Chef John Folse)

PREP TIME: 1 1/2 Hours
SERVES: 6

COMMENT:
This dish is most commonly eaten as an entree. However, try cutting it into vegetable-size portions and serving in place of a potato dish.

INGREDIENTS:

* 3 medium-sized eggplants, split lengthwise
* 2 eggplant, peeled and cubed
* 4 cups shrimp tails
* 1/4 pound butter
* 1 cup onions, diced
* 1/2 cup celery, diced
* 1/2 cup red bell pepper, diced
* 1/4 cup garlic, minced
* 1/2 cup tomatoes, diced
* 1/2 pound ground pork
* 1/2 pound ground beef
* 1 cup rich chicken stock
* salt and cracked black pepper to taste
* 1 1/2 cups seasoned Italian breadcrumbs
* 3/4 cup grated Parmesan cheese

METHOD:
Pre-heat oven to 375 degrees F. Boil all eggplant in lightly salted water until tender. Remove and cool under tap water. Using a metal spoon, scrape meat from inside of the halved eggplants, being careful not to tear the shell. Save the shells to be stuffed later. Add this scraped meat to the uncooked cubed eggplant and set aside. The cubed eggplant has been added to ensure that enough vegetable will be available at the time of stuffing. In a four-quart sauce pot, melt butter over medium-high heat. Sauté onions, celery, bell pepper, garlic and tomatoes approximately 10-15 minutes or until vegetables are wilted. Add ground pork and ground beef and slow cook until golden brown and each grain of meat is well separated. Add small amounts of chicken stock, should the meat mixture become too dry during cooking. When mixture is browned, add eggplant and continue to cook an additional 30 minutes until vegetables, meat and eggplant are well blended. Remove from heat and season to taste using salt and cracked black pepper. Gently fold in river shrimp and sprinkle breadcrumbs into the mixture to absorb most of the liquid. Using a metal cooking spoon, stuff shells with cooked eggplant mixture, dividing equally between the six shells. Sprinkle additional breadcrumbs and Parmesan cheese on top of stuffed eggplant and place on baking pan. Bake until breadcrumbs and cheese are golden brown.

Deep Fried Oysters and Shrimp (From Mike Graham)

PREP TIME: 1 Hour
SERVES: 6

COMMENT:
Deep frying is still quite common in the South. With the introduction of "lite" oils, the technique seems to live on forever. I feel it is necessary to include my own frying technique since so many customers request it time and time again.

INGREDIENTS FOR BATTER:

- 1 egg
- 1 cup milk
- 1 cup water
- 4 tbsps yellow mustard
- salt and cracked black pepper to taste

METHOD:
In a 1-quart mixing bowl blend all ingredients well. Set aside.

INGREDIENTS FOR FRYING:

- 2 dozen freshly shucked oysters
- 21-25 count shrimp, peeled, tail on and deveined
- oil for deep frying
- 4 cups yellow corn flour
- 2 tbsps granulated garlic
- 2 tbsps salt
- 2 tbsps cracked black pepper
- 1 tsp cayenne pepper

METHOD:
Using a home-style deep frying unit, such as a Fry Daddy, heat oil according to manufacturer's directions. A high quality vegetable oil or peanut oil should be considered. Corn flour, a double-ground, yellow cornmeal, may be found in the gourmet section of most food stores or as a pre-packaged fish fry such as Zatarain's. Combine corn flour, garlic, salt and peppers, blending well to ensure seasonings are evenly distributed. Dip oysters and shrimp in egg batter and then into seasoned corn flour. Deep fry, a few at a time, until they float to the top of the oil and are golden brown. Continue the process until all oysters and shrimp are done.

Crab and Asparagus Quiche (From Chef John Folse)

PREP TIME: 1½ hours
SERVES: 12-16

COMMENT: Maybe real men don't eat quiche, but moms love it! For Mother's Day, make your mom this very easy to make, rich quiche filled with succulent crabmeat and tender asparagus. She will love you more then she already does, if that's even possible.

INGREDIENTS:

* 1 cup back fin crabmeat
* 1 cup claw crabmeat
* ½ cup asparagus tips, cut into ½ inch pieces (see method)
* 24 whole asparagus spears about 4" long
* ½ cup bacon, cooked crispy and chopped
* 1½ cup shredded Swiss cheese
* ¼ cup minced onion
* ¼ cup minced red bell pepper
* 4 eggs, beaten
* 2 cups half and half
* 1 tsp salt
* ½ tsp chopped fresh thyme
* 1/8 tsp cayenne pepper
* 2 (9-inch) unbaked deep dish pie shells

METHOD:
Preheat oven to 425 degrees F. Grasp asparagus spear with two hands, holding the floret in one hand and the stem in the other. Gently bend spear until it snaps. Discard stem end. Repeat with entire bunch, reserving 24 whole spears. In a saucepan, bring a quart of water to a rolling boil. Add all asparagus and poach until crisp-tender, about 2 minutes. Drain asparagus and set aside to cool. Divide bacon, cheese, onion, red bell pepper, crabmeat and asparagus tips and sprinkle evenly into each pie shell. In a medium bowl, whisk together eggs, half and half cream, salt, thyme and cayenne. Pour egg mixture evenly into both pastry shells. Place 12 whole asparagus spears in a starburst shape on top of each pie with florets pointing out from the center. Trim stem ends of asparagus if necessary. Bake for 15 minutes. Reduce oven temperature to 300 degrees F and bake for an additional 30 minutes or until a knife inserted 1 inch from edge comes out clean. Allow quiche to sit for 10 minutes before cutting into wedges.

Shrimp and Macaroni Casserole (From Justin Wilson)

1 1/2 pounds macaroni
4 tsp salt
1 tbsp onion powder
1 tsp garlic powder
2 tbsp olive oil
1/4 tsp cayenne pepper
2 pounds shrimp, peeled and deveined
2 tbsp Louisiana hot sauce
one 16-ounce bottle mild picante sauce

Bring a large pot of water to a boil, then add the macaroni, salt, onion and garlic powders, olive oil, and cayenne and boil the macaroni until tender. Drain.

Mix the macaroni, shrimp, hot sauce, and picante sauce together and pour into a casserole dish. Cook in a preheated 350-degree oven for 1 hour.

Baked Salmon Stuffed with Alaska Shrimp (From Justin Wilson)

One 20-pound salmon, cleaned   (See note below)
Louisiana hot sauce to taste
Salt to taste
Juice of 1 large lemon
Ground cayenne pepper to taste
Salt to taste
¼ cup peanut oil
2 pounds peeled and deveined shrimp, chopped
½ cup chopped fresh parsley
1 lemon, thinly sliced
1 teaspoon dried mint

Preheat the oven to 350 degrees. This can also be cooked outside on your barbeque pit. Rinse the salmon, pat it dry, and sprinkle with salt and pepper. In a medium-sized saucepan over medium-high heat, heat the oil and sauté the green onions, parsley, and mint until the onions are tender, about 10 minutes. Stir in the hot sauce, lemon juice, and salt, then add the shrimp, stir and remove from the heat, Stuff the shrimp mixture into the cavity of the fish. Top with a sliced lemon, wrap the salmon in foil, and bake in a flat baking pan 1 to 1½ hours
NOTE: Other fish can be used, such as catfish, trout, or sea bass.

Broiled Shrimp A La Justin (From Justin Wilson)

1/4 cup olive oil
1 stick butter or margarine
2 tsp. Worcestershire sauce
1 tsp Louisiana re hot sauce
3 lb raw peeled shrimp
salt
Ground cayenne pepper
1 cup Sauterne wine or dry white wine

1.) Preheat the oven to 350 degrees.
2.) Put olive oil in bottom of baking pan, and chip butter into it. Place in oven until butter is melted. The take pan out and add Worcestershire sauce and hot sauce. Mix well.
3.) Place shrimp in single layer into the mixture, and salt and pepper them.
4.) Pour wine into pan, using approximately 1 cup or as much as is needed to half cover the shrimp.
5.) Bake in the preheated oven for 20 minutes. Then place in broiler until shrimp begin to brown. Baste frequently.

Crawfish Maque Chou (From Justin Wilson)

½ cup olive oil
1 cup dry white wine
1 cup chopped onion
1 cup water
1 cup chopped onions
1 teaspoon finely chopped garlic
¾ cup chopped bell peppers
Salt and cayenne pepper to taste
1 tablespoon dried parsley or 1 cup chopped fresh parsley
1 tablespoon steak sauce
4 cups corn cut and scraped off the cob or canned whole kernel corn, drained
2 pounds crawfish tails, peeled

Heat the olive oil in a large frying pan over a medium fire, then cook the onions, bell peppers, and parsley, stirring, until the onions are clear and the peppers are cooked. Add the corn and stir real well, then add the wine, water, and garlic. Stir in the salt, cayenne, and steak sauce, reduce the fire to low, cover, and cook until the corn is done, about 20 minutes. Add the crawfish and bring to a boil. Lower the fire and cook for 10 to 15 minutes.

Fried Oysters (From Justin Wilson)

Peanut oil
3 dozen shucked oysters
2 cups corn flour
2 teaspoons salt
1 teaspoon onion powder
1 teaspoon celery powder
½ teaspoon garlic powder
Cayenne pepper to taste

Fill a deep fryer three quarters full with peanut oil and heat to 350 degrees. Drain the oysters and place on paper towels to dry. Combine all the dry ingredients in a bowl and mix well. Dredge the oysters in the dry ingredients, knocking off any excess, and fry in the hot oil a dozen at a time until done. Drain on paper towels

Shrimp and Crab Stew (From Alex Patout's)

Ingredients:
3 cans (10 ounce) whole peeled tomatoes or 4 cups fresh tomatoes peeled and chopped
5 cups medium-colored roux
5 medium onions
3 medium bell peppers
3 celery ribs
5 pounds medium raw shrimp in shells heads on (or 3 pounds, heads off),
1 dozen live blue or other medium crabs
1 tablespoon salt
1-1/2 teaspoons ground black pepper
1 teaspoon ground white pepper
2 teaspoons ground red pepper
4-6 shot Tabasco
1 cup chopped green onions
1 cup chopped parsley

Instructions:
For this recipe I like to use Ro-tel tomatoes, because of the peppers that they have mixed in. Drain the tomatoes and put them in a bowl. Break them up with your fingers. Heat the roux over medium-high heat, add the tomatoes, and cook until the mixture is mahogany-colored, stirring often. Coarsely chop the onions, bell peppers, and celery, add them to the roux, remove from the heat, and let sit until the vegetables are soft and the roux is cool enough to touch, stirring occasionally (this will take a good half hour). While the roux is> cooling, remove the heads from the shrimp and peel them. Remove the claws from the crabs. Put the crab claws and shrimp heads and peels in a 10-quart stockpot and add 6 quarts water. Bring to a boil and boil slowly, uncovered, over medium-high heat for 45 minutes. Strain the stock, return to the pot, and set aside. Heat a large kettle of water to boiling, add the crabs, return to the boil, and cook exactly 1 minute. Drain and let cool. Clean the crabs and cut them in half lengthwise, then again horizontally (with your knife parallel to the back) to expose the meat. Bring the stock to a boil over medium heat, then add enought roux to make a thick sauce, a little at a time, stirring frequently (the sauce should drop from a spoon in thick beads). Add the salt, peppers, and Tabasco. Let simmer for an hour or more, stirring occasionally. Add the quartered crabs and cook for another 45 minutes, then add the shrimp and cook for 10 minutes. Add the green onions and parsley and simmer 5 minutes more. Serve in bowls. Don't forget the French bread! Serves 8-10.

Crab Cakes (From Alex Patout's)

Ingredients:
1 cup (1/2 pound) butter
2 teaspoons ground red pepper
3 large onions chopped coarse
1 teaspoon ground white pepper
2 bell peppers chopped coarse
2 teaspoons ground black pepper
2 celery ribs chopped coarse
2 pounds crab meat (white or claw)
1 to 2 cups crab fat (optional)
1/2 loaf French bread (day-old)
Juice of 3 lemons or 1/4 cup lemon juice
2 cups water or seafood stock
1/4 cup Worcestershire sauce
1 cup chopped green onions
1 tablespoon salt
1 cup chopped parsley
1/2 cup bread crumbs

Instructions:
Melt the butter over medium-high heat, add the onions, bell peppers, celery, crab fat, lemon juice, Worcestershire, and seasonings. Cook, stirring occasionally, until the vegetables are very soft (45 minutes or more). Add the crab meat and cook 5 minutes longer.

While the vegetables are cooking, slice the bread thin and place it on a cookie sheet in a low oven (200 degrees F) to dry out - this will take up to 30 minutes (don't let it brown). Place the dry bread in a bowl and work in enough stock or water to make a very thick mash.

Reduce the heat under the vegetable-crab mixture to low, mix in the bread mash, and continue to cook, stirring constantly, until the mixture is completely homogenized. Remove from the heat, stir in the green onions and parsley, and let cool. Once cool, add as much of the bread crumbs needed to tighten the mixture. Refrigerate for at least 2 hours. (If you live in a warm climate, it's a good idea to speed up the cooling process by transferring the hot mixture to a shallow pan and placing it directly in the refrigerator. In this case, tighten with the bread crumbs prior to refrigeration.)You can prepare the mixture up to 4 days in advance. It also freezes well.

Shape mixture into patties. Coat completely with additional bread crumbs and deep-fry in vegetable oil until brown, about 2 minutes.
Serves: Yields 6 to 8 patties.

Shrimp or Crawfish & Goat Cheese Crepes (From Muriel's Jackson Square)

Sauce

* 1 oz. yellow onion, diced
* ½ oz. bell pepper, diced
* 1 oz. tomato, diced
* ¼ t garlic, chopped
* 1 t Creole seasoning
* 4 oz. crawfish tails or 50 ct. shrimp
* 1 oz. white wine
* 1 oz. unsalted butter
* 1 t of oil
* Salt and pepper to taste

Crepe Stuffing

* 3 oz. goat cheese
* 2 oz. cream cheese
* ½ t shallot, chopped
* ½ t chives, chopped
* ¼ t salt
* ¼ t pepper
* Mix all ingredients together pipe into crepes and roll up

Directions:
Place oil in sauté pan over medium high heat, add onions and bell pepper, sauté until softened. Add tomato, garlic and creole seasoning. Sauté 30 seconds. Add crawfish or shrimp sauté 30 seconds more, then add the white wine. Reduce slightly then add butter. Salt and pepper to taste, pour over warmed crepes.

STUFFED BELL PEPPERS (From Olivier's)

6 large green peppers (blanch lightly)
2 pounds lean ground beef
3/4 pound small shrimp (diced)
1/2 pound ham (diced)
1 loaf stale french bread (broken into fairly small pieces)
1 whole egg
1/2 cup green bell peppers (chopped medium)
1/2 cup green onion (chopped medium)
1/2 cup celery (chopped fine)
1/2 cup chopped parsley
1 cup yellow onion (chopped medium)
1 tablespoon garlic powder
1 tablespoon thyme leaves
1 tablespoon whole sage leaves
1 teaspoon white pepper
1 tablespoon salt
1 teaspoon basil leaves
Cayenne pepper to taste (exercise caution, cayenne is 8 times as hot as black pepper)

In a large baking pan, wet bread with warm water. Pour off excess water, then add ground beef, garlic, thyme, sage, salt, parsley, egg and peppers.

In a seperate pan, saute yellow onion with green seasonings until lightly done (clearing), then mix with the above. Even the surface across the pan without compacting. Cover the top of the mixture sparsely with bay leaves (laurel leaves), then place pan into preheated 350 degree oven. After thirty minutes stir mixture thoroughly, bringing the bottom of the pan to the top. Total cooking time: 1-1 1/2 hours. Yield: 12 peppers

TROUT MEUNIERE WITH SHRIMP & PECANS (From Brigtsen's)
Yield: 2 servings

Ingredients:

* 2 eggs
* 2 cups milk
* 2 cups all-purpose flour
* 5-6 teaspoons Chef Paul Prudhomme's Seafood Magic seasoning
* 2 5-ounce speckled trout filets
* ½ cup vegetable or peanut oil
* 5 tablespoons softened unsalted butter, in all
* 6 medium-sized peeled fresh shrimp
* ½ cup roasted pecan pieces
* 2 Tablespoons thinly sliced green onions
* ¼ teaspoon minced fresh garlic
* ½ teaspoon Lea & Perrins
* 6 Tablespoons shrimp stock
* ½ teaspoon lemon juice

1. In a mixing bowl, add the eggs and whisk until frothy. Add the milk and whisk until thoroughly blended. Transfer the egg/milk mixture to a shallow pan and set aside.
2. In a separate shallow pan, add the flour and 4 teaspoons of the seafood seasoning. Blend well and set aside.
3. Heat the oil in a large (12") skillet over medium-high heat. Season both sides of the trout filets, lightly and evenly, with the seafood seasoning. (Use about 3/4 teaspoon per filet).
4. When the oil is hot, dredge the trout filets in the seasoned flour, then the egg/milk wash, then back again in the flour. Carefully place the battered trout filets into the hot oil. Cook the fish, turning once, until both sides are brown and crispy, 2-3 minutes per side.
5. Transfer the fish to a sheet pan lined with paper towels to drain. Set aside and keep warm while you make the sauce:
6. Discard the oil, reserving any browned bits of flour in the bottom of the pan. Return the skillet to the stove over high heat.
7. Add 1 Tablespoon of the softened butter and cook, shaking the skillet constantly, until the butter turns dark brown, 10-20 seconds. Add the shrimp and cook until the outside of the shrimp turn pink, 1-2 minutes.
8. Add the pecans, green onions, garlic, and ¼ teaspoon of seafood seasoning. Cook, shaking the skillet constantly, for 10 seconds. Add the Lea & Perrins, stock, and lemon juice. Bring to a boil. Add the remaining 4 Tablespoons of butter. Cook, shaking the skillet constantly, just until the butter melts into the sauce and becomes fully incorporated. Remove from heat.
9. To serve, place 1 trout filet on each plate and top each filet with 3 shrimp and ¼ cup of sauce. Serve immediately.

Louisiana Oyster Pie (From P & J Oyster Company)

Ingredients
1 pint oysters
1 Tbsp. butter
5 slices finely chopped bacon
1/2 cup chopped green onions
2 cloves chopped garlic
salt and pepper
1/2 chopped onions
2 Tbsp. lemon juice
1 small box sliced mushrooms
1 dash cayenne
1/4 cup flour
1/4 cup chopped parsley
1/2 Tsp. salt
2 cups biscuit dough (rolled thin)

Instructions
Cook bacon in frying pan until crisp. remove bacon, drain and crumble. Reserve 3 tablespoons on bacon fat. Sauté in bacon fat, mushrooms, onions, green onions. Cover and simmer for approximately 5 minutes or until tender. Blend in flour, salt and cayenne pepper. Stir in oysters, bacon, parsley, and lemon juice. grease a 9 inch pie plate with butter. turn oyster mixture into pie plate. Top with biscuit dough. Make several slits in top to allow for heat to escape. Bake in oven at 400 degrees for approximately 20-25 minutes, or until dough is golden brown.

Oyster and Crawfish Pasta (From P & J Oyster Company)

Ingredients
1 pint of oysters
1/2 lb. of crawfish tails
1 pinch of saffron
3/4 pint of heavy whipping cream
1/4 tsp. garlic powder
3 green onions
1/2 tbsp. onion powder
1/2 medium tomato - cut in small pieces
1/4 stick of butter of margarine
1 pinch of cayenne pepper
1/2 pack of vermicelli pasta

Instructions
Sauté , in butter, green onions, tomatoes, garlic powder, onion powder, cayenne, in a large pan, for about 5 minutes on a low flame. In a sauce pan heat oysters on medium low flame until oysters curl, (about 3-4 minutes). Pour off oyster liqueur and save oysters until later. Stir in cream and saffron on a high flame, stirring continually until sauce thickens. Add crawfish tails and oysters. Salt and pepper to taste. Shrimp or lump crabmeat can be substituted for crawfish. And either or all seafoods can be used.

Trout Marguery (From Galatoire's)

1 (2 1/2-pound) trout

1 tablespoon olive oil

1 cup water

2 sticks [1 cup, or 1/2 pound] butter

3 egg yolks

Juice of 1 lemon, strained

Salt, pepper, and cayenne

12 shrimp

2 truffles

1/2 can mushrooms

Skin and fillet trout and place the folded fillets in a pan with olive oil and water. Bake in a hot oven [400 degrees F.] about 15 minutes.
To make Hollandaise Sauce: Put beaten egg yolks and lemon juice in a double boiler over hot water and gradually add melted butter, stirring constantly until thickened. Add seasoning, shrimp, truffles, and mushrooms, cut into small pieces, to sauce and pour over fish and serve.
Serves 2.

BON APPETIT

NOTES